By the Word of Their Testimony

"And they overcame him because of the
blood of the Lamb and because of the
word of their testimony…"
Revelation 12:11

Blessings will Come and Overtake You

Book 10

Erin Thiele

Cover Design by Dallas & Tara Thiele • NarrowRoad Publishing House

By the Word of Their Testimony

Blessings will Come and Overtake You

By Erin Thiele

Published by:
NarrowRoad Publishing House
POB 830
Ozark, MO 65721 U.S.A.

The materials from Restore Ministries were written for the sole purpose of encouraging women. For more information, please take a moment to visit us at: **EncouragingWomen.org** or **RestsoreMinistries.net**.

Unless otherwise indicated, most Scripture verses are taken from the *New American Standard Bible* (NASB). Scripture quotations marked KJV are taken from the *King James Version* of the Bible, and Scripture quotations marked NIV are taken from the *New International Version*. Our ministry is not partial to any particular version of the Bible but **loves** them all so that we are able to help every woman in any denomination who needs encouragement and who has a desire to gain greater intimacy with her Savior.

ISBN: 1-931800-72-3
ISBN 13: 978-1-931800-72-3

Contents

Introduction

Your Divine Appointment

"I was **crying** to the LORD with my voice,
And He **answered me** from His holy mountain"
—Psalm 3:4

Have you been searching for marriage help? It's not by chance, nor is it by coincidence, that you are reading this book. God has heard your cry for help in your marriage dilemma. He predestined this DIVINE APPOINTMENT to give you the hope that you so desperately need right now!

If you have been told that your marriage is hopeless or that without your spouse's help your marriage cannot be restored then this is the book you need. Read this over and over so you will begin to believe that God is MORE than able to restore ANY marriage, including YOURS!

We know and understand what you are going through since WE, and MANY others who have come to our ministry for help, have a restored marriage and family! No matter what others have told you, your marriage is NOT hopeless We KNOW, after twenty five years of ministry, that God is able to restore ANY marriage, even YOURS!

If you have been crying out to God for more help, someone who understands, then join our Internet Restoration Fellowship to help you see your marriage through to restoration during your rebuilding phase of your journey Since beginning this fellowship, we have seen more marriages restored on a regular basis than we ever thought possible!

So, if you are really serious in your desire to restore your marriage, then our fellowship is the answer. For more information or to join, go to our website RMIEW.com. We would love for you to be a part of our Restoration Fellowship!

Who are we and what are we hoping to do?

Restore Ministries helps those who have found themselves in a hopeless situation: couples whose spouse is in adultery, has left, has filed for divorce, or any other seemingly impossible marital situation. These broken people have often sought help, but everyone (many times even their pastors) have told them their marriage was hopeless. However, we not only believe that no marriage is hopeless – regardless of the circumstances—we know they aren't. That's why we offer hope, help and encouragement through our website, our Restoration Fellowship, and a variety of resources including a variety of newsletters to spiritual feed and uplift you daily!

In 2001, Restoration Fellowship was birthed to minister more effectively to the needs of those seriously seeking restoration. Within a year the fellowship grew to over 400 committed members and increases daily with members from all over the world.

Restore Ministries has never sought advertising or paid for placement in search engines but has instead grown by word of mouth. We also take no support from anyone but the individuals themselves who are seeking restoration so that we are never told we must comprise sharing His full truths. Though often ostracized by the established church, because of those who have cried out to God for help when their own church, pastor family and friends who offered them no hope or support, we have given them hope and we have become an oasis in the desert for the desperate, the hurting, the rejected.

Often accused of being extreme, radical, out-of-balance or legalistic, the message in all our resources is founded firmly on the Word of God only, encouraging those seeking restoration to live the message that Jesus proclaimed, beginning with the familiar Beatitudes.

RMI teaches the good news of God's Word to bring healing to the brokenhearted, comfort to those in pain, and freedom to prisoners of despondency and sin through the truth of His Word, giving them the hope that is "against all hope" through the Power of Jesus Christ, the Mighty Counselor and Good Shepherd.

Our site and our resources minister to the hurting all over the world with the intent of creating a deeper and more intimate walk with the Lord that results in the hurting healed, the bound freed, the naked clothed, the lost saved and broken marriages restored We minister to women from more than 15 countries including Switzerland, Hong Kong, New Zealand, Sweden,

Philippines, Brazil and Germany, with large followings in Australia, Canada, and Africa. Our books have been translated into Spanish, Portuguese, Tagalog (Filipino), Afrikaans, and French. Also Slovakian, Chinese, Russian, Italian and some Hindi.

Jesus said that you "will know them by their fruits" that's why this book and all our *By the Word of Their Testimony* books are filled with testimonies of hopeless marriages that were restored marriages that give glory to God and to the Power of His Word Our *WOTT* books are growing at such a phenomenal rate that we were once unable to keep up with getting them published. Now we have a full team devoted to keeping up.

If you have any doubt about the validly of our ministry, you won't after reading this and our other awesome books. Each will show you not only hopeless marriages that were restored, but more importantly, it will show you men and women who have been completely transformed into God-lovers and are now committed on-fire Christians, many of whom were saved through this ministry.

Below is a small sampling of the letters of gratitude that Restore Ministries has received. Please note when you read the letters that they give all the praise and glory to the Lord. This ministry was founded and continues to grow on the premise that "if He be lifted up, He will draw all men to Himself" and "the Lord will share His glory with no man."

"Let Another Praise You" Proverbs 27:2

"When I arrived here, I was dejected and aware that my sins made me lose my family, then with the book on restoration, it made me hope for my marriage again. As much as people say she will never come back, I trust God. He has a promise for each of us. He made me change completely, I am becoming the husband that my wife dreamed of, and God's will shall be done!

Dear God, I thank You for everything You have done in my life! I will be a testimony of Your love as Your fisherman, because You took me out of the abyss and brought me back to life. I will not depart from You, because only You are Lord and Savior. I praise and glorify you, I love you, my God!"

~ From Jeyelson in Tocantins, who is married

"I've learned, I've grieved, I've let go, I've repented, I've gotten confirmation after confirmation, and I've grown. The best thing to come out of this is my restoration with my beloved. I've never in my life heard the expression Heavenly Husband, but I'm so grateful I have now. I have found what my heart was longing for and what has been missing all these years. Thank you Erin for your ministry! Thank you my beloved for your faithfulness, patience, provision, protection, and love. I will love you always."

~ From Kristi King in Texas

"Prior to RMI, I had decided to push my EH to divorce so I could have control of something. Through RMI I learned to let go and allow God to work on my behalf. I now run to Him with anything and everything.

Sweet friend, I know your pain. Like the website says, there IS hope at last. You are lost and He has led you here. Get to know Him. Become a bride. It may sound strange at first for we are not taught this way, but with every testimony you will see how abundant are the lives of his brides. Learn all His truth and you will be set free from pain and destruction. Don't delay. He is knocking on your door. Will you answer?"

~ From Rut Ester in Florida, who is married

We put this book and all our *Word of Their Testimony* books together because we believe that as you spend some time reading these incredible and awesome testimonies of seemingly hopeless marriages that were miraculously restored you will be encouraged and know without a doubt...

NOTHING IS IMPOSSIBLE WITH GOD!!

Nothing is Impossible
with God!

"Looking at them, Jesus said,
'With people it is impossible,
but not with God;
for all things are possible with God.'"
Mark 10:27

*"And they overcame him because of the blood of the Lamb and because of the **word of THEIR testimony**, and they did not love their life even to death." Rev. 12:11.*

The following testimonies are filled with miracles of men and women who took God at His Word and believed that "nothing was impossible with God!" Those who have had the miracle of a restored marriage have several things in common. All "delighted themselves in the Lord" and He gave them "the desires of their heart." All of them "hoped against hope" when their situation seemed hopeless.

All of them "fought the good fight" and "finished their course." All of them were determined "not to be overcome with evil" but instead to "overcome evil with good." All were willing to "bless their enemies" and to pray for them that "despitefully used and persecuted them." All "turned the other cheek" and "walked the extra mile." All realized that it was "God who removed lover and friend far from" them and it was God who "made them a loathing" to their spouse. All of them understood and believed that it is NOT the will of man (or woman) but the "will of God" who can "turn the heart" whichever way He chooses.

All refused to fight in "the flesh" but chose to battle "in the spirit." None were concerned to protect themselves, but trusted themselves "to Him who judges righteously." All of their trust was "in the Lord" because their trust was "the Lord." All released their attorneys (if that was part of their testing) since they "would rather be wronged or defrauded." All of them "got out of the way of wickedness" and "let the unbeliever leave" since they "were called to peace." All refused to do "evil for evil or insult for insult." All loved their spouse who may have been unfaithful because they knew that "love never fails."

This is the same journey that the Lord took me on back in 1989. That year I made a promise to God that if He would restore my marriage to my husband, I would devote my life to telling others about Him and His desire and ability to restore ANY marriage no matter what the circumstances. The Lord was faithful and restored my marriage, suddenly, two years later after a divorce. (Yes! AFTER a divorce!) Now I faithfully, with the Lord's continued help, love, support, and guidance, spread the GOOD news that nothing—NOT A THING—is impossible with God!

It is important to know that our ministry was FOUNDED to help all those who were told by pastors and Christian friends that their situations were HOPELESS. Those who come to us for hope are facing a spouse who is deep in adultery, who has moved out (often in with the other man or woman who committed adultery with), who has already filed for divorce or whose divorce has gone through. 99% of those who come, come alone for help since their spouse is not interested in saving their marriage, but is desperately trying to get out. Over 95% claim that they are Christians and most are married to Christians.

Over half are in some type of Christian service and many of the men who are involved with other woman are pastors who have left not only their wife and children, but their church as well.

If you, or if someone you know, is facing devastation in their marriage, there is hope. Read these awesome testimonies that prove that God is MORE than able to restore ANY marriage—even YOURS!

Chapter 1

Alison

"Be strong and courageous.
Do not be afraid or terrified because of them,
for the Lord your God goes with you;
he will never leave you nor forsake you."
—Deuteronomy 31:6

"My Parents died, My Children Taken, My Husband Left"

Alison, how did your restoration actually begin?

My journey began exactly two years ago, when my husband decided to leave me, and he took everything he had with him—all his clothes in the closet—in short, everything that was his was gone when I woke up one morning. But I wasn't that concerned, because prior to this (when he'd been angry) there were many comings and goings for him to blow off steam. In fact, this happened maybe twenty or thirty times over the course of our marriage. This time, it was a huge blow, because it happened only two months after I lost my mother and father in a car accident.

I was a new believer, trusting Him after the loss of my parents, when I was able to find peace. After losing my parents, and especially after I found the Lord as my Saviour, my marriage went from bad to worse, with many more betrayals on his part that added to everything I was going through. It was when I could no longer stand the pain that I sought and gave my life to my Saviour, and I sincerely thought that everything would be resolved overnight. But it was a huge assumption on my part. Everything became complicated!

My mother had died; my father was gone; my children were taken from me to live with relatives, and suddenly my husband left. Altogether, due to the immense pain, I thought I'd go crazy. That's when I began looking for help and when I found the RMI. Like so many testimonies, I also read the book How God Can and Will Restore Your Marriage, in two days. Then I began a deep intense study, going through all your free online courses. Although it was my marriage that led me here, when I arrived all I wanted was to know everything! I wanted to know about a Husband who would never leave or forsake me and love that would heal the pain that I thought would be my undoing. And so it was, with much crying, much pain, my journey began.

How did God change your situation, Alison, as you sought Him wholeheartedly?

The transformation began when I let myself be carried by the hands of my God—when I met and became the bride of my Beloved. When His company was enough for me; that's when I realized that He made me happy, that it was only His love that I needed. I delighted in the presence of the Lord! I opened my eyes each morning with anticipation, rather than dread or fear. Rather than recoil to face another day, I waited with joy for each event that I knew awaited me, a gift from my Lover! I knew He would do the miracle, miracles, in my life! In the eyes of the world, my earthly husband was living in another state with OW (other woman), and he was "happy." Adding to my losses, even his relatives turned their backs on me, when we had been very close since we were very small.

But I said to my God, "My Beloved, HH (Heavenly Husband), I am happy in Your company, and I do not believe in appearances; Your Word says that the adulterous woman will become bitter like wormwood and that there is no peace where You do not live."

What principles, from God's Word (or through our resources), Alison, did the Lord teach you during this trial?

The principles were to let go of the church, so we can make our Saviour our Heavenly Husband, in order to find rest for our souls. Once you have this, you have everything you could need or want, and it's when you can let go of everything, because nothing else compares. I wanted to "extract the precious from the worthless" (Jeremiah 15:19, NASB).

What were the most difficult times that God helped you through, Alison?

The hardest moments during my journey was when his family turned their backs on me, because they were the only family I had. Of course, not having my children with me was also hugely difficult. What drove me to discover this journey is when my EH (earthly husband) found and began flaunting the OW, when I was in such pain. I felt not only the loss of my husband—but immense loss for my children and his entire family. It was very painful, but the Lord, my Husband, sustained me.

Alison, what was the "turning point" of your restoration?

The turning point happened after I'd let go of the church, and God used a sister who'd come to see me in my home, because she said God had spoken to her and told her to go and tell me. She said, God said, "Tell my servant that I am taking that man out of the filth and the mire, and I am bringing him home, because that is how I do it; I honor those who honor Me and believe in Me."

She said that she knew it was for me, when God spoke, because everyone had been talking and praying for me, ever since I'd left the church in order to gain a stronger relationship with the Lord. She arrived unannounced, coming from the evening service and drove over that same night.

As Erin says, prophecy, someone saying they have a word for you, is only true when it confirms what He already has spoken to us. This was exactly what He'd been telling me for weeks, so I knew that it was He who had sent this messenger—even though I didn't need Him to send anyone, because I'd heard it from His own mouth, from His own Word.

Then the very next day, at noon, my husband called and told my son that he was leaving the OW. He said, call your mom and tell her we're all coming home.

Tell us HOW it happened, Alison. Did your husband just walk in the front door? Alison, did you suspect or could you tell you were close to being restored?

When my son called me, I was more startled by the fact that my son contacted me than by what he called to tell me—that my whole family was returning home. However, it was a full month after this call from my son that my restoration happened.

A week after I heard nothing and no one came, my EH called saying he wanted a divorce. He said he wanted it, because he'd been away from home for almost two years, and he couldn't see how this would work. I'd read both Facing Divorce and Facing Divorce, Again, so I was prepared to be enthusiastic and agree, so I said, "Divorce is fine with me, if that will make you happy. Just let me know when you need me to sign." Instead of him filing for divorce, just as the course says will happen, he started calling me and saying that he wanted his family back; he wanted our family together; he never once stopped thinking about us as what made him happy.

So two years, two months and two days from when I'd lost my family, they returned home. It wasn't easy at first, but I had my HH, so I was determined He would remain first in my life and heart. I would often go off to be with Him, and it was easy to tell I "had" a Lover.

Would you recommend any of our resources in particular that helped you, Alison?

I recommend RMI and all your resources to everyone. I recommend this ministry to someone every single day, and I bring it up with whomever I am speaking to. I open my phone and show them where to go to find healing of every sort. Most people in our community know what I went through and are amazed by the woman I am today.

I thank Erin from the bottom of my heart for sharing her journey with us and setting us off on a path where we find much more than restoration for our marriages. Finding my Lover is what I'd always missed and what I hope each woman who comes here finds.

After my Saviour and my Heavenly Husband, it is Erin who is responsible for all the good that God has done to me, by the ways she lovingly guides us and points us to His Word and having a relationship with Him. No church does that; it's all so perfect.

I have no doubt that Erin is an angel that God put here for each of us, to help us and give us courage. "God, please reward Erin; I know that there is a very special heavenly mansion You have prepared for her and that one day she will live in the largest one, in order to entertain all of those she's helped."

"Erin, you have accumulated unimaginable treasures in heaven, souls that are no longer weeping but are devoted to their Husband in a way no one else explains. The Lord is pleased with you. Thank you! Thank you! Thank you!"

So sisters, believe me; believe that God is faithful; He will watch over you and will fulfill His Word.

Would you be interested in helping encourage other women, Alison?

Yes. I'm interested in helping other women.

Either way, Alison, what kind of encouragement would you like to leave women with, in conclusion?

Never speak badly about anyone; do not socialize; give this up and focus only on your most precious relationship—with your Heavenly Husband. Feed on His Word, and read it as love letters and what He promises to do for you, too.

Beloved, believe! God is Faithful. He is! Much more than having my earthly husband back, it is precious to have my beloved Husband, my Lover! Dear sister, you can have this right now. I lost everything, and everyone in my life, and yet I found happiness, joy unspeakable, love so deep it felt as if my heart would burst. I know it can be the same for you!!

Know that He hears your prayers! Know that every tear is stored up in a bottle. Dear bride, He lives; He loves us; He cares; He protects! Give yourself wholeheartedly to Him. He is wonderful! Enjoy this time in your desert with Him, because He's all sweetness; He's all calming; He's entirely perfect. Beloved Ones, discover that the desert is a place of refreshment in the Lord. Thank You! Thank You, my Beloved! I love You! I need more of You than the air I breathe! I do not want to breathe if I do not have You!!!

Chapter 2

Jana

"When there are many words, wrongdoing is unavoidable,
But one who restrains his lips is wise."
—Proverbs 10:19

"Never Give Up on Your Restoration!"

Ministry Note: This Restored Marriage Testimony is very special to me. Even though I've never met Jana, when I heard she was one of the members of the WhatsApp group started by Valentina, who was once a dear close friend, our Portuguese Minister and then was suddenly taken from us, after sowing seeds of hope into rich soil that are yielding a crop of good fruit as you will read. ~ Erin

Matthew 13:23—
"And the one on whom seed was sown on the good soil, this is the man who hears the word and understands it; who indeed bears fruit and brings forth, some a hundredfold, some sixty, and some thirty."

Jana, how did your restoration actually begin?

I was a rebellious daughter and my husband had a rebellious streak as well. I had no real relationship with God when I was young. I was looking for other things in the world to make me happy and fulfill my needs of abandonment and depression, which were the result of an unstructured and disrupted family growing up.

After I married, I realized there was a void in my life and soon I found out that I was being betrayed by my husband. I felt rejected, humiliated, really thrown into the mire and I understood what says in Psalm 55:12-14: "For it was not an enemy that reproached me; then I could have borne it: neither was it he that hated me that did magnify himself against me; then I would have hid myself from him: But it was you, a man mine equal, my guide, and mine acquaintance. We who took sweet fellowship together, and walked unto the house of God".

The foundation of my life slipped from under me and in despair, I wept because I couldn't understand why my marriage was over. There were long painful years of crying, but also healing and deliverance.

To compound my distress, I was pregnant when my mother passed away, and I was angry with God because He had not healed my mother. I felt more and more alone.

We were blessed with a beautiful son, yet, I was very much alone at home and only took care of our son. I forgot that my husband was there and that I had a life besides just being a mother. Furthermore, I did make room for my husband to be a father, to take care of our son because I feared he'd become aggressive with him and was afraid of what he could possibly do to our child. I forgot that sometimes he was loving, I was too hurt to see any of his good qualities.

My husband told me he didn't want to go to church anymore because I had to stay with our son in the Children's Church Room and he couldn't understand. He said that he did not want to have a child, he didn't like that he did not sleep, and that he was very nervous due to these things. To cope he went back to drinking and doing many things that separated him from God.

I continued to go to church, mostly I cried. I simply didn't have time to search for God in a quiet and alone time. I wanted to know Him, to listen to Him, but I did not know His Word, and I had never been taught how to seek Him. But when I found and read the book How God Can and Will Restore Your Marriage, I got to know Him intimately and His Word and then I was able to see myself and my sins.

How did God change your situation, Jana, as you sought Him wholeheartedly?

I made so many mistakes before I found RMI that I saw my marriage die and could not do anything. I was too busy and stuck in my millions of sins. I did not renounce nor repent of them, I did not see them, I only saw the sins of my husband and others, I was selfishly thinking only of my personal salvation and happiness.

I even hoped that my EH would be punished. I wanted to be happy and without looking and "loving my neighbor as myself." I thought I was the best in everything, I thought I was the most spiritual because I went to church. I often preached to my husband and became his "holy spirit." I tried to force him to go to church so he would change.

In addition to all this, I lived in lies, I lied about the values of things, I lied to please, I lied to avoid discussion, I lied that I had won something when in fact, I had bought myself nothing but... devastating lies.

I was very impatient, I fought over a dirty glass, his clothes thrown on the floor, argued when my EH drank. In addition, I was gossiper (it was not about spreading rumors, but I talked about the sin of others and did not look at my own). I refused to be submissive to my husband or anyone else in authority. I would not take orders from anyone nor being contradicted by others.

I judged everyone and made myself a victim. I took what was not mine, for example. I ate at the supermarket and didn't pay for it or I kept the extra change that the cashier gave me when it was the wrong amount. I had a lot of anger, unforgiveness, etc ...

So God started to transform me and also to change my situation. I was able to see all my sins when the scales fell from my eyes.

Alone in my secret room, I went through the courses provided by RMI—courses that were my key to victory—He took me to my neighbor who became my prayer partner, as she was going through a situation similar to mine.

What principles, from God's Word (or through our resources), Jana, did the Lord teach you during this trial?

Won Without a Word, because before I wanted to win with a multitude of words.

"In the multitude of words there wanteth not sin: but he that refraineth his lips is wise". Proverbs 10:19-29

I went to church 1 or 2 times a week, but I didn't know God and what it was like to have an intimate relationship with Him. I had religion, but I didn't have God.

Letting go of my church and learning how to be a wise woman and that our first ministry is our home. \o/

I often rejected my husband in all situations, anytime I was very angry, hurt and sad. Knowing about the Intimacy while Still Married was fundamental for our restoration.

What were the most difficult times that God helped you through, Jana?

I saw my husband drinking more and more, smoking, using drugs, being aggressive towards me and my son. Every year it got worse inside my house, and I being a fool talked about his sin to everyone and to his mother (the worst mistake I made), and I always said, "I can't take it anymore", "I'm tired" and just didn't pray anymore. I wanted to disappear and go back in time to erase everything before all this started—back to my wedding day.

But in the midst of so much pain, I lived with the best and greatest Love in the world, I lived my own restoration and God rewarded me with a restored marriage. :) In fact, I will live the restoration daily, until I meet My Beloved Heavenly Husband here and for all eternity.

You can be happy in all areas of your life when you first find joy in God and meet your Beloved Heavenly Husband.

"Thou wilt shew me the path of life: in thy presence is fullness of joy; at thy right hand there are pleasures for evermore." Psalm 16:11

Jana, what was the "turning point" of your restoration?

While I was fasting and praying I started looking for restored marriages on the internet and putting on the armor of God—daily and in prayer, I also covered my husband in prayer instead of in my words to Him. I really prayed without ceasing.

I found the book How God Can and Will Restore Your Marriage and read it in 3 days and then I prayed the prayers found at the end of this book.

I started the courses but I decided to do Course 2, because I thought: "as I already read the book, I don't need Course 1." But then I came back and I did course 1 and saw that it was very different from the book.

I was transformed daily, I no longer looked at my husband's sins, or what he did, I declared that my joy came from the Lord and I could live contentment in any situation. I let go of attending church and started to meet the Lord in my prayer closet instead. I spent hours studying and praying after work and my focus was to be transformed. Everyday I cried and asked God for help, I did not fear bad news or what I was seeing, I lived by faith towards my victory.

One day I got home, I was doing course 2, and I went to bed, I prayed and said: "I don't want the restoration anymore, I just want You, Lord. Enough, I will live to serve You!" I started to take care of myself more, I dressed up and went for walks with my son, I started to enjoy his company (because before sadness wouldn't let me!). And I liked to teach him things, and wow, it was wonderful! My Beloved has dried my tears, He has become my Husband, and the best Husband! Everything was perfect between us!

Tell us HOW it happened, Jana? Did your husband just walk in the front door? Jana, did you suspect or could you tell you were close to being restored?

While I was restored from inside out, my husband was also changing and looking at me differently. The scales began to fall from his eyes, and he became more affectionate, asking me for forgiveness for what he had done and we are together as a family again!

He stopped taking drugs, drinking alcohol, or causing fights and and he went back to church, sometimes he took us with him.

My husband is more and more transformed and is a new man. I am grateful for everything and I wait for God to finish the good work that He started!

Would you be interested in helping encourage other women, Jana?

YES! I became a RMI partner, and I know that this way I can help women from all over the world to learn what I learned here.

I also have an encouragement group on WhatsApp, where we share the lessons of the courses and support each other in prayer as ePartners. I am also part of the "Beloved Children of the Father and Go Restoring Ministry", which are branches of RMI. We are women who meet in person and online to study the book, A Wise Woman :)

The important thing is to live His love abundantly and share that love and faith with everyone to whom He sends us.

Either way, Jana, what kind of encouragement would you like to leave women with, in conclusion?

Dear friend, don't forget that it is a spiritual battle! Even after the restoration, sometimes, my EH (earthly husband) arrived home drunk, but I trusted Him. I waited on my EH, and served him, took off his shoes and took care of him. Calmly, I sat with him and just talked, I didn't judge him. Other times, he went out to concerts and pubs, and as Erin said, so did I, I went with him, but I went praying in my spirit! But quickly he stopped, my husband didn't want to do these programs anymore, thanks to my Beloved because I honored rather than judged my EH!

"And whosoever shall ask you to go a mile, go with him two." Matthew 5:41

Don't be a spectator, live the restoration! Take care of the children of God and then He takes care of you! Never give up on your restoration!

Chapter 3

Marabel

"Likewise, wives, be subject to your own husbands,
so that even if some do not obey the word,
they may be won without a word
by the conduct of their wives"
— 1 Peter 3:1

"I Didn't Want to Be Married"

Marabel, how did your restoration actually begin?

My relationship started about 8 years ago, we started as friends and in a short time we were in love. He was my first boyfriend and then after yet another fight, it all ended. I thought he loved me and that he could never leave me, but I was very wrong. I was nasty to him so how could I ever think he wouldn't leave me some day? I was quarrelsome, controlling, contentious, proud, and most of the time I was cruel, abusive really. I find it fascinating that women believe we can be abusive in what we say but if a man does it to us, it's entirely different and unexceptable.

I knew I really loved him but my pride was huge. I didn't treat him as someone of any value. So in this fatal fight, I stayed weeks without contact and was shocked that when I finally got in touch, he didn't want to come back. I found out later that he was already in a relationship with another woman. It was a blow I didn't see coming. Like he'd stabbed me in the heart. I was inconsolable, I begged, I cried, but all the pleading was in vain. He said he was happily involved with the other woman and everything I did only made the situation worse. I even went to talk to the other woman, but that only increased her interest in him. Every day after work he went to her house, every day without missing a day. He didn't care about anything but her, he was blind and even a bit bewitched.

How did God change your situation, Marabel, as you sought Him wholeheartedly?

After I saw everything fall apart, I went into utter despair, I did not eat, I did not sleep. In my depression as I cried out to God, I began to remember what I heard so many people say, that God who could do anything. Nothing was impossible with Him. Although I believed that He existed I did not believe that He would be so alive, so present in anyone's life, and had no understanding that He loved me. So I cried in desperation and begged God to help me, to let me know Him so He wouldn't let my dreams die this painful death.

Guided by God, I knew it had to be Him, I went to a website and saw a phone number of a person who was going through this situation. I sent a message and she replied and told me about the book (how God can and will restore your marriage) and soon after searching I found it and found my way to RMI. Like a stream in the desert for the first time I thought I may not die after all. It was like God put a balm on my wounds. At first, it hurt a lot, I thought I would never be able to endure so much pain, but I flung myself at the feet of the Lord, cried out for relief, and little by little I discovered the truth in His Words and I managed to get up and begin to live again. God treated me as His own. I learned about His Son and witnessed how He is faithful in everything He promises and gives you more than your own dreams.

What principles, from God's Word (or through our resources), Marabel, did the Lord teach you during this trial?

I remember that I spent hours praying that God would remove him and take him away from OW (other woman) grasp. Praying that he would love me again. I wasted a lot of time until I got to know God, then I became my Heavenly Husbands' bride. I felt so much joy in His presence, I heard praises and rejoiced—in the joyful times I praised Him, and I learned to praise in difficult times even more. That's when my life story started to change. Once I was seeking my HH above everything else, at all times. Brides you must trust and trust and then trust Him some more.

What were the most difficult times that God helped you through, Marabel?

The worst moment was letting go. I was reluctant to let God work. I thought that if I disappeared that he would forget me, but I began to understand that staying in touch made him loathe me and want to escape even more from my grasp. God needed to show me my errors after gently trying to coax me to let go.

It all happened one night when I went over to his house. He'd asked me to say away but I went anyway and just walked inside the unlocked door. When I refused to leave, he left, he texted me saying he said he wasn't going to come back, that he was going to sleep at her house. That night, listening to all these hurtful words again, left me raw. I left and went to my parents' house because I didn't know what to do and that's when I decided to leave it to the Lord—because I saw that I didn't have the strength and could do nothing.

Marabel, what was the "turning point" of your restoration?

The turning point happened after I got to know God, meditated on the Word, poured myself into each of your courses, prayed, fasted, cried a lot at the feet of the Lord, and struggled not to look at the situation. I was receiving confirmation that God would restore but that's when I no longer wanted it. I know that this is often when marriage restoration happens, but I wasn't married. I had been living with my boyfriend who had no intention of marrying me (and while living together I didn't even want to be married either). The turning point was A Wise Woman, specifically when I got to Chapter 7, "Chaste and Respectful."

This chapter got my attention when I read, "We are told that respect is something we should demand from others. We are told that we should have respect for ourselves. To learn the true meaning of respect, let us look for a deeper understanding. Our husbands are to be won "by the behavior of their wives, as they observe [our] chaste and respectful behavior" (1 Pet. 3:1). The word respect is defined in the dictionary as "special esteem or consideration in which one holds another person"! It is not what we demand for ourselves!"

What is chaste? The word chaste as: clean, innocent, modest, perfect, pure. Webster's Dictionary defines chaste in two ways: 1. Innocent of immoral sexual intercourse (fornication); innocent of a manner of speech (reread lesson 4, "Kindness Is on Her Tongue.") 2. Dress, modest, restrained, pure, unadorned.

I began to search for help as a single woman, a brand new single woman who was now washed pure and a woman who didn't want to be polluted. Having a HH (Heavenly Husband) made me realize I didn't need a man in my life and when it was Him I wanted. I yearned for more time with Him, I wanted to trust Him and I wanted to wait until I was married to be with a man. I so wanted to be treated kindly now that I had a gentle and quiet spirit and had experienced His gentle love. In the process, I also moved back in with my parents to help with any temptations and that's when God restored my relationship with them!

Tell us HOW it happened, Marabel? Did your husband just walk in the front door? Marabel, did you suspect or could you tell you were close to being restored?

After I moved back in with my parents and found such contentment wanting to remain single and pure is when my boyfriend began texting me. After ignoring him, I realized I needed to block him. Since I let go of Facebook, there wasn't another way to connect to me, so that's when I found out he went to where I used to live. I would never have imagined being pursued by a guy who always has women chasing him. He always said it was beneath him, but nothing is impossible with God.

It took a couple of weeks for him to track me down (I'd changed jobs too). He showed up at my parents' door one night and I told my sister to tell him I wasn't available to come to the door. The next morning when I left for work I got to the sidewalk and there he was waiting for me. He asked me what was wrong, why was I avoiding him and when I didn't really say anything, he said he'd missed me. I still didn't say anything, then he said something I thought I'd never hear him say. He said he was sorry for running after the other woman, that he should have come back when I'd asked and that he was ready to be together again. He asked if he could move in with me at my parents or did I want to come live with him at his mom's house?

From the moment I saw him standing there I started asking my Darling to know what to say, to speak through me, to give me the words to say and to remain strong and resolute. To not fall into temptation. When I opened my mouth to speak I heard myself say, "Thank you for all that you said, but I am not the same person you left. Not coming back was the best thing that could have happened to me. I found Someone else too, a relationship that makes me so happy and Someone I don't want to lose." Then I turned and hurried away to catch my bus that had just pulled up. As it drove off I saw my boyfriend just standing there staring, stunned.

So my restoration is with my parents and most importantly with God. And when it's the appointed time, I will build my new relationship on the Rock. I will remain pure and vow to treat my earthly husband as a wife with a gentle and quiet spirit

Would you recommend any of our resources in particular that helped you, Marabel?

Even though the book HOW GOD CAN AND WILL RESTORE YOUR MARRIAGE is for women who are married, it really helped me a lot to know God had everything under His control. But I first recommend reading A WISE WOMAN to really make sure that all you believe is founded on the Rock. I also recommend the bible app to read through the bible and listen as you read. All your courses are amazing as are the praise reports and devotionals.

Would you be interested in helping encourage other women, Marabel?

Yes, probably helping single women who think themselves married.

Either way, Marabel, what kind of encouragement would you like to leave women with, in conclusion?

The desert we go through is used to get to know Him, God, then to know our Lord who washed us with His blood, who came into the world to forgive, not condemn any of us. Knowing the Lord as a HH is wonderful, I wish I had this relationship sooner but trust I will be in love with Him and Him with me forever. Forever with Him. Thank You God for choosing me, for having restored my heart, and opening my eyes and plucking me from living in sin and despair. I believe that Your work in my life will continue long after You bring the right husband into my life. I promise to seek You and not look for any man but allow you to choose. I hope the most wonderful blessings flourish in your lives, dear sweet sisters. I love You, thank You Father and my most Precious Love.

Chapter 4

Myra

"Let your eyes look directly ahead and
let your gaze be fixed straight in front of you."
—Proverbs 4:25

"It Ripped My Heart Open"

Myra, how did your Restoration Journey actually begin?

My journey began when I found out that my husband was having an affair, and I mistakenly thought that once I uncovered his sin, that he would repent and ask my forgiveness. That is not what happened, what actually happened was that it became worse - because now I knew and he wanted to stay with her and it became an open marriage. He did try initially, but that was for a short while, and then he would leave in the middle of the night and return in the morning - and it tore my heart out each time. We had cameras in the garage and around the house for security and I would see his car gone or pulling out, going to her house, and it ripped my heart open and I would cry and be in such grief that I could not eat or think straight. I would check the cameras all night until his return at about 5 am, and then start the day. He would get some rest and start a late workday with some hours of sleep. It was during this time that I found RMI, and he helped me so much! To hear that Erin had been where I was, in the same pain, with children - and it inspired me - to follow her advice and to most of all PRAY!

How did God change your situation, Myra, as you sought Him wholeheartedly?

God changed me so deeply! I felt like He was watching over me, that he was helping me to transform and become a better person. The experience was so awful and painful, but through this I have become closer to Him and understand so much more than I thought I did before. I was a pharisee, but through fire, I was able to burn off the cords that bound me and now I was free to pray with a joyous heart!

What principles, from God's Word (or through our resources), Myra, did the Lord teach you during this trial?

So many principles! Thank you so much, Erin!

The chapter on Contentious Woman was so inspired and opened my eyes to myself and how difficult a wife I had been. The "Kindness on Her Tongue" helped give me the principles I needed to be a better wife and person. Won without a Word, gave me hope, to know I did not have to DO anything, just follow Him. And finally, a Gentle and Quiet Spirit gave me direction on how to move forward - what to work towards for myself.

What were the most difficult times that God helped you through, Myra?

God helped me most when it was time for my husband to go, for me to let go and pass my earthly husband to Him. It was a very hard time for me. I showed my support and faith by helping my earthly husband put together what he needed to move out, i.e. pots/pans/towels/sheets. I turned it all over to God and found peace.

Myra, what was the "turning point" of your restoration?

It was when I knew that I could let go - and that God would take care of me and that He was my Heavenly Husband and that He was all I needed. That I could continue without my earthly husband and find my happiness and support with my Heavenly Husband!

Tell us HOW it happened, Myra? Did your husband just walk in the front door? Myra, did you suspect or could you tell you were close to being restored?

The day of moving out, when I had completely let go, when I let him make the choice (before I had always talked him out of it) - he had his car packed and movers scheduled and the apartment rented. And he did not leave! He texted me and said he would go for a drive and he came back to me and wanted to stay!

During his drive, I prayed and prayed, prayed for peace and for His will to be done. And he texted me that he would NOT be leaving! Thank you, dear Lord!

Did you suspect or could you tell you were close to being restored?

I did suspect something because he had said he would leave 2 times before - and I had been crazy with anxiousness and would talk to him and reason with him.

But this time, he was serious and went to look for apartments and I was at peace! I could not understand it - I was expecting the anxiousness, the crying, the pleading - BUT - I was overcome with a peace I had never felt before. I was able to pray without anxiousness - and I actually was able to sleep the nights before I knew he was going to leave. I believed that God was comforting me, and filling me with peace for when my earthly husband would walk out the door.

Would you recommend any of our resources in particular that helped you, Myra?

Of course - How God Can and WILL restore your marriage!! All of the website, all the emails - such a blessing to women that are in this predicament. Thank you, Erin! I send you warm thoughts and blessings from Bellevue, WA. You are a blessed woman - so much thanks!

Myra, do you have favorite Bible verses that you would like to pass on to women reading your testimonies? Promises that He gave you, Myra?

"Trust in the Lord with all your heart and lean not on your own understanding; in all your ways submit to him, and he will make your paths straight." Proverbs 3:5-6

"Never will I leave you; never will I forsake you." Hebrews 13:5

"Create in me a pure heart, O God, and renew a steadfast spirit within me." Psalm 51:10

"Love always protects, always trusts, always hopes, always perseveres. Love never fails. But where there are prophecies, they will cease; where there are tongues, they will be stilled; where there is knowledge, it will pass away." 1 Corinthians 13:7-8

"Let your eyes look directly ahead and let your gaze be fixed straight in front of you." Proverbs 4:25

"And my God will supply all your needs according to His riches in glory in Christ Jesus." Philippians 4:19

"He has brought down rulers from their thrones, And has exalted those who were humble." Luke 1:52

"Those who sow in tears shall reap with joyful shouting." Psalm 126:5

"Rejoice in the Lord always; again I will say, rejoice!" Philippians 4:4

"Wait for the Lord; be strong and let your heart take courage; Yes, wait for the Lord." Psalm 27:14

Would you be interested in helping encourage other women, Myra?

Yes

Either way, Myra, what kind of encouragement would you like to leave women with, in conclusion?

Believe!

Believe that the Lord cares for you, that He sees you in your room, He sees your tears and your anguish. He sees the grief that takes over you night and day. Have faith that He is working, through your husband, to make you a better person. Be humble. Be contrite and let the Lord work thru you. Believe that you will reap joy with your husband when the time is right.

Chapter 5

Elda

"The LORD will fight for you,
while you keep silent."
—Exodus 14:14

"I Started Letting God Fight my Battles!"

Elda, how did your Restoration Journey actually begin?

My restoration journey began when I had unknowingly become a contentious woman. I would constantly criticize my earthly husband and tell him to leave if he wasn't happy. Well, one day he decided to leave. I cried and begged him to not leave me and our daughter. But that only made him angrier towards me. I ended up reading a book on how to save my marriage, through the flesh, but as we know that didn't help. Then I saw Erin's book appear on my feed. I read it so fast and realized how wrong I was. I stopped looking at my earthly husband's sins and really took a hard look at myself.

How did God change your situation, Elda, as you sought Him wholeheartedly?

I became to truly depend and love the Lord. My Heavenly Husband was truly the only one I wanted and needed. Every time I thought I couldn't go on any further, He would encourage me to keep pushing forward and to trust Him. Every time I thought I wouldn't make it financially, He always provided and spoiled me with gifts. I never lacked anything. I was a Christian but not one who actually had a relationship with Him. The more I leaned on my Heavenly Husband, the more I realized I didn't need my marriage to be restored.

What principles, from God's Word (or through our resources), Elda, did the Lord teach you during this trial?

I think the biggest thing is truly understanding that God is in control of every situation. I always needed to remind myself of Exodus 14:14. I started letting God fight my battles so I could remain calm and keep my eyes fixed on my Heavenly Husband.

I have found such an overwhelming amount of love for the Lord now than ever before. I was so far from being a godly woman and since reading Erin's books, I've begun to change and crave the Lord's words. I would love to be able to have a connection with other women who share similar beliefs.

I have always attended church growing up but never had a personal relationship with the Lord. It is since finding this ministry that I have truly found the Lord again. I now understand He loves me and I love him. I am learning something new every day and I love it.

What were the most difficult times that God helped you through, Elda?

The hardest part was when my earthly husband made the decision to get his own apartment, but I knew he was actually moving in with the other woman. Then he drove her car to pick up some of his items. But thankfully my Heavenly Husband had prepared me to know something big was going to happen, so I was able to get through it calmly.

Elda, what was the "turning point" of your restoration?

The turning point was when I finally surrendered my marriage and earthly husband to God. I said whatever you want to do with my life, go ahead. A few days after we celebrated my daughter's birthday, my earthly husband broke down and said he missed me and loved me still. We became intimate again. This went on for a month before he could make the decision to leave the other woman and move out of his apartment.

Tell us HOW it happened, Elda? Did your husband just walk in the front door? Elda, did you suspect or could you tell you were close to being restored?

I could feel it was close to him coming home because he kept getting more and more depressed from being away from his family. He also kept complaining more and more about the other woman.

Yes, I could tell I WAS close to being restored because the closer I kept getting to the Lord, the more my earthly husband wanted to be with me. It truly happens when you let go of everything and let God work.

Would you recommend any of our resources in particular that helped you, Elda?

I would recommend all of RMI's resources. They all were helpful and led me to truly have a relationship with my Heavenly Husband. He is all I truly need in my life. No man can ever compete. But I am beyond thankful for what God has done in my life.

Elda do you have favorite Bible verses that you would like to pass on to women reading your Testimonies? Promises that He gave you, Elda?

"The Lord will fight for you; you need only to be still" Exodus 14:14

Would you be interested in helping encourage other women, Elda?

Yes, I would love to encourage other women.

Either way, Elda, what kind of encouragement would you like to leave women with, in conclusion?

I would say never give up as hard as it gets. Every moment is worth it. Enjoy every moment through the journey because this is the best time you will have with your Heavenly Husband. Words simply can't explain how thankful I am for God for taking my earthly husband away and restoring me back to Him. Then restoring my earthly husband back to me. God cares about you and He cares about your marriage. Let Him work and stay calm. Truly rest in His peace and love there is nothing that compares.

Chapter 6

Janice

"I lift up my eyes to the mountains—
where does my help come from?
My help comes from the Lord,
the Maker of heaven and earth."
—Psalm 121:1-2

"We were Simply 'Separated' Inside the Same House"

Janice, how did your restoration journey actually begin?

I want to start by saying that since I was always a contentious, bossy woman, know-it-all, among other things (I'm so thankful I am not any longer) it took me a long time to realize that my marriage was in bad shape. The company I worked for also went bankrupt, which further contributed to my stress, complaints, murmuring and disgust for things. My husband, who was always extremely affectionate, loving and patient, started to become strange and cold with me. He'd spend a lot of time on his cell phone and I started to get very bothered by it. However, despite complaining about it, I never touched his things, until one day by chance when I took his cell phone out of the charger to put mine on, I saw an affectionate message from another woman. My world fell at that moment even though he swore it was no big deal and deleted the message.

From then on our marriage was in chaos, the fights were constant until he asked for a separation, saying that "we" didn't work anymore. I, in my foolishness and immaturity, left the house—giving the enemy a key to our front door—quickly entering in to further destroy my marriage. I stayed at my mother's for a month, but we didn't lose contact. I confess that I ran after him, pursuing him, because I didn't know about Letting Go.

After a month I came home and saw his message again with other woman. At this moment I went into total despair, I felt used, ridiculed and everything ugly that you can imagine. That was the week we would have been married for ten years. So, I screamed, I told the whole family, I felt like the victim "the poor thing that always did everything in the relationship and was betrayed." That same day I moved back in with my mother.

How did God change your situation, Janice, as you sought Him wholeheartedly?

I was totally desperate, because I really saw that my marriage of ten years was falling apart and that despite so much arrogance, I wanted my marriage back. I loved my husband too much. So one night of crying and suffering I started searching the internet for restored marriages. At first I found things that didn't help me much and just made me more depressed, showing me that there was no hope. Until I found the RMI. THANK YOU GOD!

I downloaded the book, How God can and will restore your marriage, but I got irritated, because I could not understand the biblical passages at all and as the book is full of the Word of God, I gave up reading it. But I continued to read the testimonies on the website. Then I started asking God to do that for me too and to please help me to make sense of His Word. I don't know how to explain it, but God took root within me that I should trust Him and not give up.

This all happened towards the end of the year and my Earthly Husband asked me to spend the New Year at his sister's house in another state. I went, even though I knew my family didn't want me there. I started to be suspicious of everything. Every time he looked at his phone I was in agony. We fought again on the day we returned home, but since I no longer wanted to be ashamed of having to go back to my mother's house for the third time, I went home with him, but we were simply separated inside the same house.

At this point, I started to seek God even more. I didn't believe what was happening to me. I read the testimonies and saw the women talking about the RYM book and I said to myself, "I need to understand what it says...." So I started reading the book again, but this time God touched me, and I understood every passage! Soon I started to see that I had destroyed my home. My heart started to be broken. The problem is that my Earthly Husband didn't want to hear from me at all. We stayed in the same house and decided that until we managed to sell the house we would live together. It was one of the most difficult moments of my life!

What principles, from God's Word (or through our resources), Janice, did the Lord teach you during this trial?

I always had difficulties with the principle of letting go, but I knew it was necessary. I avoided him rather than always trying to be "around" and I stopped catering to him, fixing meals, doing his laundry. At the same time I began to pray non-stop, as I had lost my job and stayed at home all day. And I fasted too. As I clung to God, reading His Word, my Earthly Husband approached me. As Erin quotes in one of the videos, I never stopped being intimate with him. I confess that I felt used many times, but I cried out to God to take those feelings away from me because I knew it was the enemy wanting to steal my blessing.

What were the most difficult times that God helped you through, Janice?

It was having to be inside the house with my Earthly Husband and sleeping in separate rooms. Knowing that he was exchanging messages with Other Woman. But God helped me and did not abandon me. It was months of crying and suffering. I missed feeling loved, but He supplied everything then once I met my Man in Finding the Abundant Life, I was able to let go because I felt loved. I stopped crying and began to be happier than I'd ever been!

Janice, what was the "turning point" of your restoration?

Erin says that when God's blessing is close, the enemy will rise up so that we will give up and it is true. I was fine, praying and fasting, enjoying my new Love. I knew that in God's timing He was going to restore my marriage. My Earthly Husband said that he had no one else and that he just wanted to separate. But I prayed to God in prayer that if there was something or someone hidden that He would show me. And my Beloved is faithful. One day, I woke up knowing that God was at my side and that it was only a matter of time for my restoration to happen. One day out of the blue my Earthly Husband said he had no more contact with the Other Woman. I was elated but then...

As I was doing my housework, I thought I should do his laundry, but as I put his clothes in the machine, inside my Earthly Husband's pants pocket was a receipt from a motel dated on the previous day. My dear ones, I don't want to expose my Earthly Husband, I just want you to show you how dirty the enemy is. At this moment I was very attached to my Man so I asked Him and He said, "Trust Me. Don't believe what you see, that is not faith."

Tell us HOW it happened, Janice? Did your husband just walk in the front door? Janice, did you suspect or could you tell you were close to being restored?

My Heavenly Husband is merciful and soooo loving. After this situation, God spoke to the heart about my Earthly Husband and he started to incline his heart towards me. He apologized to me and said he was sorry and that I was the right woman for him, the only woman for him. He said that if I could really forgive him that we could move to where his parents lived and start a new life. My friends, my restoration came in the midst of a great tribulation. When I began my journey I cried a lot to God for my Earthly Husband to say that he loves me again and to begin wearing his ring again (he hadn't worn it for years). And it's beginning to happen! He began to say he loves me. And as for the ring, he told me it was too tight on his finger and then told me at the Easter service... "Let's both buy new rings."

Would you recommend any of our resources in particular that helped you, Janice?

Yes. I mainly recommend the book, How God Can and Will Restore Your Marriage, Courses, Devotionals and Testimonies (they were the resource that wouldn't let me give up).

I also must thank Erin from the bottom of my heart for sharing her life with me and with thousands of people who need encouragement and would be lost without the hope she devotes her life to give us!

Would you be interested in helping encourage other women, Janice?

Yes

Either way, Janice, what kind of encouragement would you like to leave women with, in conclusion?

I would like to ask you who are in the midst of the blazing fire not to give up. God is greater than anything you can be feeling. I thought my marriage was hopeless, but with God nothing is impossible. I am now living in a new state, living a new life, but this new life is centered around the Lord. I need to improve a lot, but I know that God will help me. Marriage is something from God, it is not His intention that your family be destroyed. And don't forget, when it starts to get worse—don't stop believing because your blessing is coming quickly!!!

"Wait on the Lord, and keep your way and you will be exalted to inherit the land; you will see it when the wicked are despicable." Psalm 37: 34

Psalm 121:1 "I lift up my eyes to the mountains— where does my help come from? My help comes from the Lord, the Maker of heaven and earth."

Chapter 7

Annie

"Truly, I say to you, if you have faith and do
not doubt, you will not only do what has been
done to the fig tree, but even if you say
to this mountain, 'Be taken up and thrown
into the sea,' it will happen."
—Matthew 21:21

"My Life Changed and I Stopped Crying!"

Annie, how did your restoration actually begin?

My RESTORED Testimony should have been written several months ago, but we ended up so busy with our new life, I forgot. But today is the day, the appointed time, because I know that many women go through similar situations and I owe it to my Heavenly Husband to share the truth. I want everyone to know that they can be sure that God changes history, He resurrects what is dead, because He is God...and it is for the honor and glory of His name I tell my story.

We lived together for 23 years, without officializing our union, never legally marrying. We have 2 daughters, and we lived in our marriage completely distant from God, even though we continually were receiving blessings from God in our lives. It's amazing that God is good to us even when we don't deserve it. We never stopped to see that He blessed us and we turned our backs on Him. We lived a sinful union full of ups and downs, betrayals, fights, arguments, and jealousy. Yes, we loved each other but without the presence of God we let the enemy act in our lives. But that all changed in October. The first great crisis hit when I discovered my Earthly Husband had a lover and without any wisdom, I acted out. I fought, cursed, I called the Other Woman, I threatened her. I continued this until he left her. In my ignorance as a stupid woman, so quarrelsome, who wanted to be in control of everything, I thought everything was resolved.

Then, in March, our financial life was hit very badly. We had our own business and we decided to open a second store to see if things would improve financially. Pure deception. Within 40 days my Earthly Husband said he didn't love me anymore, said he wanted to be single, to take care of his own life. I was blindsided. I was shocked by what I became over the years. So, I agreed, I even thought it was a good idea— after all, I was free of that boring marriage. I could do anything and everything I wanted now. Do what I hadn't done for so many years. So I was happy, making plans.

Then, my joy turned into a nightmare, it lasted a few days, maybe 5, 7 days. I don't know for sure, but God touched me that it was not what HE wanted for my life. There was utter despair, I felt inside my heart that I was wrong, that I couldn't lose my family, my daughters would suffer, and the pain was so great. So I told my husband that I didn't want the separation, that it wasn't the best choice, but at this point he had already decided he wanted out and there was no going back. I lost my ground, my footing. I realized how much I loved my husband and how much I loved my family, but by that point he was already involved in the evil that took over his life. I discovered then that he had already found a girlfriend.

Then without any direction, I started doing everything I shouldn't have, I started chasing, calling, watching, chatting, fighting, and one thing that was worse, I put his whatsapp on my PC to spy on him. One day I read everything he wrote and what he received from messages. Oh, God, I suffered such horrors, don't ever do that, and I just sank into the deepest pain, and without the presence of God the enemy took over my life. I didn't eat, I didn't drink, I didn't sleep, I just cried, I wanted to kill myself, I wanted to become a homeless person, everything bad I thought about doing. So I lived for two months like this, sunk in the mud, destroyed, a rag, pain hitting me all over the place, but I didn't remember that God existed. Until one day God had mercy on me and in one of those fits of crying it came to my mind to look for a church and so I did. I went aimlessly to church after church. Remember that I didn't go to church, I had never once opened a Bible to read it. From then on God started to come into my life. Praise the Lord.

I started going to church, I was crying, I cried the whole service and I came back crying. And my happy husband was with the Other Woman, would leave early from work, did not talk to me all day, came home to sleep each night, then stayed with her at the weekend, came home late, and so the months went by. When I started going to church, soon after I met a woman, a Godsend. God put a prayer woman in my life, who started to accompany me, pray for me, pray with me, asking God to send me hope. I had none, none at all. Then one day I was browsing the internet and I found this blessed Ministry. My life changed and I stopped crying!

How did God change your situation, Annie, as you sought Him wholeheartedly?

Reading the Book How God Can and Will Restore Your Marriage I saw what I had become, what my life had become, and when the scales began to fall from the eyes, it was very painful because I discovered that I was responsible for the destruction of our family. After this is when God started to take care of all my hurts. I had never kneeled to pray, and every time I did this simple act, it was painful, because I saw my mistakes, but I was learning. God used a Wise Woman and taught me how I had to to be as a woman, wife, mother, daughter and sister.

What principles, from God's Word (or through our resources), Annie, did the Lord teach you during this trial?

I read the RYM book twice, watched all the videos several times, read each of the lessons, and read the Bible a lot. During and through these resources, God spoke to me a lot, mainly through the Word. I let go of the church, because I'd stopped crying after He led me here. Now, I trusted Him.

What were the most difficult times that God helped you through, Annie?

There were so many difficult times, like when he said that he did not love me, that he loved Other Woman, that I was nothing to him, that I was only the mother of his daughters. Maybe even worse was the weekend that he came home, and saw that he had gotten dressed, put on cologne and went out with her. That night I stayed at home on my knees weeping at the Lord's feet, without even the strength to stand up, but then God held me in His hands and I felt a peace overtake me.

And also as the months passed, God said that He would do a miracle in my life, that I had to believe but things only got worse, my husband told everyone that he was going to marry her, because as we were not married on paper, nothing prevented that he married her. At that point, he was totally blind, beside himself, he no longer remembered that he even had daughters, he was totally in the hands of the enemy. But I told God from the beginning that I was going to marry him, and each day that passed got worse. God taught me to trust but there was one phase of my journey I still needed to pass through.

Annie, what was the "turning point" of your restoration?

In November, my husband was with the Other Woman almost entirely. He made it a point of saying that he did not love me, and began treating me like nothing when he was in our store. He left early, he arrived late. I always fixed him dinner, because over the months I learned to treat him well, I didn't ask, he didn't charge, he didn't care, I had his clothes that were always ready for him to wear, the house was always clean, the food was always made, and I acted as if nothing had happened. I had also moved away from all the people who could bring me information that could make me suffer. I was not going to anyone's house, much less to his family. I started living at home and that's when I met and fell in love with my Heavenly Husband. I finally discovered my First Love.

That's when I was ready to face the final blow. We financially lost everything, the store closed, God closed all doors for him, and even without me seeing anything, understanding anything, God was acting on my behalf. As I said God said he would do a miracle. And when everything seemed to have no way out, God entered and I was blessed with a Lover. God honored me because my daughters never lacked anything even though we'd lost everything.

Tell us HOW it happened, Annie? Did your husband just walk in the front door? Annie, did you suspect or could you tell you were close to being restored?

At the end of November, out of nowhere, my husband came to me and said that he had realized that he loved me, and on the same day he returned home. Three weeks later we got married, and the next day we were baptized in water. And for the glory and glory of God we are together and living our lives together for HIM!!

Would you recommend any of our resources in particular that helped you, Annie?

I recommend to everyone I meet, the RYM book, all your videos, all your lessons, study the testimonies because these are what gave me strength. Each time I read one, I cried a lot but I said, if God did it her life He can do it in mine too. Reading the Bible is very important, so is fasting, letting go of your church and finally, the most essential thing is to surrender to God, even in the midst of so much pain, it is the only way. Lastly, find your First Love in order to heal.

Would you be interested in helping encourage other women, Annie?

YES for sure! In the same way that I needed help, I am willing to help, to pass on my testimony, to say, "Look, have faith, God will do in your life what he did in mine!" "And Jesus answered and said to them, 'Truly I say to you, if you have faith, and do not doubt, you shall not only do what was done...but even if you say to this mountain, "Be taken up and cast into the sea," it shall happen'" (Matt. 21:21).

Either way, Annie, what kind of encouragement would you like to leave women with, in conclusion?

First, never give up on your family, don't give up on your husband, because our fight is not against the flesh, but what is behind all this. An enemy who wants to destroy families! Your family is worth surrendering to the only One who can change our history! The fight seems to have no end, it seems that the pain will consume you, but God is in control of all situations. Today I have my husband who is devoted to the church and being a spiritual leader. And my daughters, the month after we were restored, they were born again and now go to church with their dad (I remain at home and am a member of Restoration Fellowship). Then two months later my daughters were baptized. So now I can say that I and my house serve the Lord, and that the glory of the second house will be greater than that of the first, so says the Lord. Ladies, God is wonderful, I live miracles in my life every day! God is Faithful. Just be in His presence and trust. Praise be to God!!!

Chapter 8

Antonella

"I will say to the LORD,
'My refuge and my fortress,
My God, in whom I trust!'"
—Psalm 91:2

"I Simply Wanted to Be Happy, Period!"

Antonella, how did your restoration actually begin?

All my life I really wanted to get married and have children. It was my dream!!! I wanted to be happy in my marriage, and I thought it would be easy. But I didn't think about giving in, or doing anything to make my marriage happy, I simply wanted to be happy, period! I got married and a month later we had our first child, and then the second and then the third...I wanted the house full of babies!!! My husband just went with the flow.

We met in church, he and I were already Christians, but with our courtship we had already cooled down spiritually. I was very arrogant, bossy, full of myself. When I met my husband he was a virgin, so I thought the best way to ensure that he was "mine" was to put his hand in the fire of sin, that way he would never betray me. Living sinfully forced him to do the right thing and marry me once I was pregnant. But once we married I was never submissive to anything!! I never knew this is what GOD says. For me, everything he said was wrong, only I was right.

To top it off, I neglected my body and gained over a hundred pounds between pregnancies. After all, what was the problem, right? Of course he would never leave me, wrong!!!

How did God change your situation, Antonella, as you sought Him wholeheartedly?

One day, I was tired of living that emptiness that I lived in, we no longer went to church, we didn't read the Bible, and we let alcohol into our house. Then, in my despair when I saw what was happening to my family, I cried out to God, and decided that I was going to seek Him. I remember lying in bed with my husband, he, with his back to me, I said, "Darling, one day God will transform our marriage and our financial life (which was already destroyed) and we will give a great testimony." Then he said to me, "Ok, sure, now let's go to sleep." My husband did not hear me, hear my heart, but God heard me at that moment.

So I started going to services alone, trying to fulfill what I'd said. I just got up and took the children one Sunday. When I asked him to come with us he said, "No, you go." This was the closest to submission I'd gotten, up until this point in our marriage—but I was way, way off from knowing that I never should have stepped in as the spiritual leader. Yet, God had pity on me.

Then He woke me up, shook me up and got my attention big time! He showed me that my husband was in adultery!!! My husband, who only had been with me, a man who was very shy and had deep rooted values. This man was talking to and involved with another woman. On the day I found out, I begged him to tell me who she was, but he denied it, until he said, "If I tell you our marriage will be over." That was enough for me to go berserk! I jumped out of the car like a crazy woman, called my cell leader from the church I was attending and told him what had happened. And you'll never imagine what he said (or maybe you will). He said to kick him out, send him away packing!

When I got home I packed his stuff and I took everything over to my mother-in-law's house (who lives next door) and told everyone that I wouldn't accept living with a cheater! I shouted it over and over. After this my husband was very cold towards me but also somewhat relieved that I had taken that sort of action. He wanted to leave me so he could spend more time with her without having to sneak around. Just like A Wise Woman title, I was the fool who tore her house down with her own hands! I played right into the enemy's schemes, what a fool!

When I got home, and realized what I had done, what a fool I'd been, it fell on me like a ton of bricks. I collapsed to the floor and oh how I cried!! What incredible horrible pain!!!! The fool succeeded in destroying her own house!!!! After three days, I was introduced to RMI through an acquaintance, who today has become a great friend. A woman who also had her marriage restored. Every day I read the book How God Can and Will Restore Your Marriage, I burst into tears, because I saw how far I was from the Lord, and I saw the answers I'd craved for years and how I'd gotten myself into this dire situation.

What principles, from God's Word (or through our resources), Antonella, did the Lord teach you during this trial?

I fought against my flesh, but at the beginning, I confess, that I faltered several times. I wanted to apply the principles like asking forgiveness, but I needed to be broken. I tried, but when I went to talk to him, to tell him how I'd messed up, I hesitated. I wept and prayed for forgiveness from the Lord and that He would help me to obey Him. The Lord gradually transformed me. God never left me alone. With love and care, He taught me and transformed me. I learned to shut up, to listen to my husband, and to be submissive even though he was not living in our house. I learned to seek the Lord, in times of pain and despair and when my flesh screamed—I ran into His arms and was calmed and relieved by His love.

What were the most difficult times that God helped you through, Antonella?

During our separation my husband denied any involvement with anyone, I did not seek to know, did not follow him, but God had already shown me that he had someone else through a dream, and that the person was a Christian. He, in His infinite love and kindness, already prepared me to know what was hidden. One day while doing my homework for my Restoration Journey courses, I heard a voice and it said, "Four months." It was so vivid that it stayed in my mind all day, and I knew it was the Lord's voice, but I didn't know what it was about. I thought in my little mind that it would be the date of my restoration, when the fourth month of separation arrived.

Instead four months was when the identity of the Other Woman would be revealed. One day, after four months of separation, my prayer partner and another friend were all ending a church-wide fast, so I invited them to have something to eat at my house. Like a fool, I'd resisted letting go of my church even though I'd studied the lesson and applied to be a Restoration Fellowship Church member, and due to my resistance the Lord had warned me, "four months." He'd given me four months to do what I knew I should, but didn't.

So on this fateful day, this other friend of mine tells me that her cell leader had just separated from her husband, he had caught her talking romantically on the cell phone with another man. At that moment I almost collapsed to the floor—I knew the other man was my husband. They had already dated as teens, and I knew my husband and her husband's cousin were close friends. She was a cell leader, and had several ministries in the church. At the time I said out loud that it was my husband, and my prayer partner at the time felt the same thing as me, but this other friend of mine did not believe me and said that I was crazy, that this super spiritual woman would never do that to me.

We didn't talk about it anymore, thankfully I let it drop, but when they left I was trembling and couldn't stop. I was in shock. Someone so close to me, someone I knew so well, we even owned stores facing each other. Oh God how would I go to work each day knowing what was going on? But despite the certainty in my heart, nobody really knew that it was my husband who was involved with her. So I gave it to the Lord, told no one else. Then things began to happen. The pastors confronted her, but she denied it and said it was someone else from another city. Stupidly I fell into the enemy's trap and asked my husband, thankfully, he denied it too, and at the same moment I knew it was wrong for me to ask him, so I simply said, "I believe you." Because as Erin says, "Love believes all things" even when we know something isn't true.

Rumors spread throughout the church, then throughout our entire city. Every day someone told me something I didn't want to know, oh, what a horrible pain. But God used it for good. This is when I let go of everything, my church, and I found my First Love! Once I had a Heavenly Husband who really was who He needed me to be, the pain was gone!

Antonella, what was the "turning point" of your restoration?

Despite the circumstances, and the immense pain I was feeling, I treated my husband with love, and as if nothing had happened. And as a result we got closer and closer. While fasting and constant prayer I watched the hate wall falling. As a result, I lost a lot of weight. Before the separation I had already lost about half my excess baby weight due to dieting and working out at a gym. After the separation I lost another significant amount. Yet during my continual fast and brokenness, the "infidelity diet that I read in Chelle's testimony on my first day here at RMI" I lost all my baby weight and it caught my husband's attention. He looked at me with admiration, seeing that I managed to get the body back to the way I looked when we were married, and also seeing how I had changed as a woman. He once told me, "You are like the person you were when we first met, only better."

Tell us HOW it happened, Antonella? Did your husband just walk in the front door? Antonella, did you suspect or could you tell you were close to being restored?

As I lived next door to him, he came to our house often after I'd changed. I made lunch, dinner, then we often had coffee in the afternoon (which I didn't do before). One day while the children were at school in the afternoon and we had already begun being intimate again after 5 months apart, I discovered I was pregnant. I was even taking the pill at my husband's request. Even so, he was very happy, making plans to return, but I knew it was because of the child I was carrying. Nevertheless, I trusted God that He would do what was best.

Then after 6 weeks of gestation, I discovered that it was an ectopic pregnancy. We were devastated. I was so sad, and ashamed. I asked God, "Do I have to go through this further shame?" And at the guidance of my husband, he asked me not to tell anyone else that I had lost the baby. He said he wanted to come home. So I obeyed him, but it was horrible for me because people complimented me on having another baby that was no longer inside me. I was very embarrassed and horribly heartbroken.

A month passed, and he didn't come home as he had promised and he also wouldn't let me tell anyone about the baby that I'd lost. It saddened me so much to lie so much, so I cried out to the Lord to find a way to get me out of this situation. Then my brother found out that I had lost the baby because it was an ectopic pregnancy and he worked in that hospital. Once he knew, everyone knew. The news spread. In fact, I really believe it was the Lord's providence. He heard my cry and my pain. So I shared what was going on with my husband and he agreed to talk about the loss of the baby. Even though he still hadn't come home, I was calm because I knew everything was in His timing.

During the procedure to stop the ectopic pregnancy, I took a very strong medication, in which the doctor told me that I would not ovulate, and I could not get pregnant again. But after only 3 months, I got pregnant again and the ultrasound showed the baby was in the womb, and perfect. I didn't find out until I was in the middle of my second trimester because I never imagined I could get pregnant.

The news that was once a cause for joy, this time was terrible for my husband. He was furious and blamed me for getting pregnant on purpose. He said things like "I said I was going to come home but you got yourself pregnant thinking I wasn't coming back just to force me."

So I just told my husband that if he wanted to come home one day, that was fine but if he didn't want to, it was also okay, that he didn't have to come back because of the baby. Things calmed down when I let him go and soon afterwards he brought his things back. When he returned, my children were euphoric. I'd never seen such happiness. Yet I kept myself from showing how happy I was.

To this day, my husband has not confessed to me everything that happened about his adultery. We talk very little about it. He does not feel comfortable, and I also understand that I don't need to or want to hear what happened. He just told me that he did commit adultery and that I might not want him anymore. He didn't go into details. It hurt me a lot before, but not at all now. What is a bit sad is that he doesn't have the courage to go to any church because of what happened, he feels ashamed.

The battle is not over yet, now the battle is against us being together. He is not yet our spiritual leader, but I kept believing that the Lord would finish the work that He started. Then just this morning he suggested we do a sort of home church. I'm excited about that. It's silly to imagine that the enemy won't continue to lurk around, looking for a breach to break us apart again. Nevertheless, my husband loves me, and he's home and we're happier as a family, living peacefully for the first time in all the 7 years of our marriage.

Would you recommend any of our resources in particular that helped you, Antonella?

I do recommend how God can and will restore your marriage and a wise woman. I recommend the lessons and videos, and the Abundant Life series. All I can say is this Ministry is such a blessing!!!

Would you be interested in helping encourage other women, Antonella?

Yes I would like to help other women. I believe I went through so much pain to be able to help someone else who is in this situation.

Either way, Antonella, what kind of encouragement would you like to leave women with, in conclusion?

Even though everything might appear to be over, and that there is no way, He will change everything, He solves everything, it is enough just to remain under His wings. "He who dwells in the shelter of the Most High will abide in the shadow of the Almighty. I will say to the Lord, My refuge and my fortress, My God, in whom I trust!" Psalm 91:1-2 He made me rest in the most horrible, terrifying moments. When I was alone with three children, He gave me peace and calmed me and told me that He was restoring my home, my life for His sake.

The pain was necessary for me to come to Him. But only in Him, by your Heavenly Husband's love, can this pain be relieved and we will be healed. Another thing, the Other Woman in which my husband got involved with, is rich, beautiful, and is very well groomed. I know my Earthly Husband thought she was an incredible woman of God, because of the positions she held in the church, everyone described her as the ultimate prize. But His Word says, "Charm is deceitful and beauty is vain, but a woman who fears the Lord, she shall be praised" (Prov. 31:30). "Delight yourself in the Lord; and He will give you the desires of your heart" (Ps. 37:4). That's the secret. Delight yourself in the Lord your Heavenly Husband!!!

Chapter 9

Alessandra

"When he would not be dissuaded,
we fell silent and said,
'The Lord's will be done.'"
—Acts 21:14

"OW Held EH Hostage During My Pregnancy"

Alessandra, how did your restoration actually begin?

I was willing to get a divorce to stop the way my husband and I were living. I thought this was my only option. So I searched on Google about the types of divorce. I saw a list of lawyers who specialized in divorce but then I was kind of curious, wondering: What does God think of divorce? My heart along with my lack of understanding made me believe that God wanted everyone to be happy and if we were not happy, it was ok to divorce. Even so, the doubt did not leave me...I decided to research about God and divorce and so I was directed to the passage in Malachi where it says GOD hates divorce. When this path was no longer an option, I started to research on how to restore my marriage and that's when my Heavenly Husband guided me to RMI.

Reading the book, How God can and will restore your marriage and then reading the Bible to confirm that what was said in it was true, convinced me I was now on the right path. Before, I didn't even know where to start, but the verses quoted in the book were essential for me to head in the right direction. In the beginning all I wanted most was for God to restore my marriage ASAP but as time went by and He healed / transformed me, I wished for all of Him in my life and no longer desired restoration. I started to love our moments together: talking to Him, singing to Him, meditating on His Word. My every waking moment was filled with utter joy. My focus changed little by little and then I began to ask for a restored marriage if this is what God wanted for our lives. I didn't want my marriage anymore! Then I began to really want my earthly husband back but with my Heavenly Husband being the center of everything in our lives!

How did God change your situation, Alessandra, as you sought Him wholeheartedly?

As I read the book, I saw all my mistakes and I went from victim to villain! I didn't know that I was so foolish, my heart was wide open and totally surrendered to the hands of my Beloved to guide me, and when I read each verse from the Word of God I was being transformed, and I fell in love with Him. I wondered how I could have lived so long without enjoying this abundant life and missing out on a life that was always available to me??? My Beloved was transforming me from the inside out, He filled me with a joy that I didn't understand because the world continued the same way but it didn't affect me anymore.

What principles, from God's Word (or through our resources), Alessandra, did the Lord teach you during this trial?

For sure, win without words! I always had to be right, I always had to have the last word, so being quiet was not easy for me. As it says in the lessons, I began fasting because it made me weaker, I didn't even have the strength to talk about anything, let alone argue. Agreeing became easy and when I saw the results, wow, I was hooked. Peace and contentment. And there was another great benefit for me because besides keeping the peace with my earthly husband and everyone I always argued with—I lost 21 kgs or 46 pounds!

What were the most difficult times that God helped you through, Alessandra?

My earthly husband began asking me for a child, we had no children because we decided when we married we would never have any. But then, as I dreamed of GOD restoring my marriage, I decided that restoration needed to come first. But my earthly husband insisted saying he wanted a child and didn't want to wait, so I decided to submit and gave everything to the Lord and thus I became pregnant.

Throughout my pregnancy my earthly husband said he would come back but he did not come back during my entire pregnancy. If I had agreed just to please my husband, rather than submitting "as unto the Lord" I would have been bitter. But there was no greater Husband or

Father to my preborn daughter than my Heavenly Husband was to me! It was a glorious pregnancy!!

Then, when I was about halfway through my pregnancy I received a call from my mother-in-law informing me that my earthly husband was involved with and had a girlfriend. I replied to her: "The Lord's will be done!" I was a little sad, of course, but I knew that the Lord was in control of everything. When I met up with my earthly husband and I didn't confront him and I didn't even mention it because I had the full conviction that God was taking care of it for me, I could see in my husband's face that he was stunned! That's when I just smiled a knowing smile because I knew my Husband was with me and smiling with me!

Alessandra, what was the "turning point" of your restoration?

It happened when I let it go completely. Whenever I needed something during pregnancy, I simply had to ask and my Beloved would give it to me! Even in the daily needs of all the small repairs that were needed in my home (I live in an old home). Each time He guided/enabled me to do it! Whenever my earthly husband and I said goodbye, he asked me to call him for anything I needed but I always preferred to look for Him, my Beloved! His mother confronted me to do something to stop her son because I was being very "permissive" with him but I always replied that only God could control a grown man. She couldn't control him as a teen, how could I control him? I also reminded her once that in our fights he complained about the lack of freedom in our relationship, so now, I wouldn't and couldn't interfere. In my heart I knew that My Beloved would do anything for me, all I had to do was pray and trust!

Tell us HOW it happened, Alessandra? Did your husband just walk in the front door? Alessandra, did you suspect or could you tell you were close to being restored?

The Lord wanted to restore my marriage at a specific appointed time. It all happened during surgery of all places!! My earthly husband told me he wanted to accompany me at the birth of the daughter. So during my delivery, which was cesarean because the baby was breech, he sat down next to me and whispered: "I'm coming home!" I was already beginning to "fade" from the anesthetic, but I remember that I replied: "You have said this so many times…" Then he replied: "But today it is for real, my bags are already in my car!" When I was discharged, we went home together, he had already moved in most of his clothes and a day later he went back for the rest when he knew the other woman was at work! He told me that the other woman had "held him hostage during my pregnancy threatening to tell everyone details of his life with her, posting intimate pictures of them on facebook." So he'd stayed away from me, but now he said he "loathed her and every harlot." PRAISE GOD only He could have done this. I had prayed these exact words just once and He did it!

I want to take this time to apologize to my Beloved for not having shared my testimony before this. Our daughter is 18 months old already! However, I know He will use this for good because I am here to say when you wait for GOD to restore, it is restored for good!

Would you recommend any of our resources in particular that helped you, Alessandra?

The book, How God can and will restore your marriage. I didn't have a Christian walk even though I was a Christian and went to church religiously. But that was the point, until I came to RMI I never had a relationship with the Lord! It wasn't spoken of in the church, nor did the emphasis reading the Bible, which is both our life's roadmap and love letters from our Beloved all rolled into one! Therefore, when I read that I should let him go and win without words, they seemed to me to be a bad joke because it was completely the opposite of what I was willing to do. But dear brides, believe! Submit! Do what His Word says, do what each lesson says to do. If you're not yet restored, go back to see what principles you chose to ignore and do them. Better yet, ask Him which you ignored and ask Him to help you do them.

Would you be interested in helping encourage other women, Alessandra?

Yes, for sure!

Either way, Alessandra, what kind of encouragement would you like to leave women with, in conclusion?

Do not give up! Many, many times I felt tired and wanted to give up. So often it "appeared" as if nothing was happening and I thought about giving up. But never forget, we live by faith not by sight. "For we walk by faith, not by sight" (2 Cor. 5:7). "The sacrifices that please God are a broken spirit; a broken and contrite heart, O God, you will not despise." Psalms 51:17

Chapter 10

Maite

"You hypocrite, first take the log out of
your own eye, and then you will see clearly
to take the speck out of your brother's eye!"
—Matthew 7:5

"God was Working for Me Without Ever Knowing He Was!"

Maite, how did your Restoration Journey actually begin?

It all started when I was 17 years old. I met my husband at church when we were both young, and while we were dating we had sex. My mom found out and together with my dad they encouraged me to get married. At the time, we were married out of obligation. It was horrible! The first year of marriage was one of many fights, sorrows and disappointments. The second year, I discovered my husband was cheating on me so I decided to do the same. I was unable to forgive him or me after that! In doing the same, being unfaithful and because I couldn't forgive, my life went from bad to worse.

Six years passed, and in the seventh and our marriage was full of problems. I was a terrible wife. I was contentious, quarrelsome, proud, jealous, possessive. During fights I always told my husband to get out. After he'd go I'd sent messages on his whatsapp humiliating him. I was so miserable and unhappy! And worst of all, I thought I was a super Christian and would not admit that this was happening to me. It wasn't fair! (I thought to myself). How hypocritical! "First remove the beam from your eye, and then you will be able to see clearly to remove the speck from your brother's eye." Matthew 7:5. Many pastors and my own family and even I thought I had married the wrong person and advised me to find someone new. Can you imagine?!? What I needed was to be different, not find someone different so I kept repeating the cycle!

How did God change your situation, Maite, as you sought Him wholeheartedly?

Well, I found RMI a few years ago. I took the first course but I didn't take it too seriously. But even then some things changed for the better in me. But I did everything wrong again and my marriage was worse than before. So when I couldn't take it anymore, I fought with my husband, I sent him several messages by cell phone and in the end I threw him out of the house. That night when my husband came home from work, I was already asleep. But before that I prayed to God saying "I can't take it anymore, God, You need to do whatever is necessary to change my marriage."

That day my husband left and didn't come back. I couldn't understand. How could my husband leave if I had prayed for God to change my situation? Because, at that time, I didn't understand that this was exactly what God used to transform us. This time too, when my husband left, he said he didn't want to talk to me and to just go ahead and file for divorce (like I always threatened) and my mom told me to go ahead, do it.

When that happened, I ran to RMI, started reading the book How God can and will restore your marriage! And began the courses that same day too. Glory to God! I found hope! Believe me, my marriage was dead. Over! My husband did not want to talk to me, we went for more than a month without speaking. It was horrible! He told my father that he didn't like me and in fact he didn't even know how he felt about me, that he was disgusted even when he heard my voice. I was devastated hearing that from my own father! There were many trials, many OWs. But God was faithful! I started to seek God and apply the principles I had learned that God was working for me silently without me ever knowing He was!

What principles, from God's Word (or through our resources), Maite, did the Lord teach you during this trial?

Let it go. Not just Let Go. The Let Go principle was very important and that's when I really began seeing changes. When I tried to talk to my husband or to get in his way, he always stayed away from me. But when I let him go, just as Erin said, he began chasing after me. Tithing to your storehouse is huge for restoration. Fasting and praying of course. And to praise God for everything good or bad!

What were the most difficult times that God helped you through, Maite?

When my husband ignored me. We rode the same bus to go to work. He didn't sit next to me, but instead he'd sit with OW and then the enemy planted several lies to my mind. There was a day that I couldn't stand anymore and I was going to give up, I was ready to call him and say "Okay, guess what? I am going to file for divorce!" But I prayed to God and He asked me to wait. The very next day my husband spoke to me again and was very kind and I realized God had turned his heart so the enemy had to mess with me. Beloved, urgency is always the cunning scheme of the enemy. God is patient!

Maite, what was the "turning point" of your restoration?

The turning point was when I gave everything to my Beloved. I no longer even cared if my marriage was going to be restored and most days I did not want restoration. I even prayed that I wouldn't be restored, because I had such peace, I had the love of my Husband. Believe me I was happy with my Beloved! But His plans are better than mine, my marriage is better than before. I've never been happier in my life. My husband said he realized he loved me and asked for forgiveness. God surprised me! My husband would never do that if it weren't for God. Never!

Tell us HOW it happened, Maite? Did your husband just walk in the front door? Maite, did you suspect or could you tell you were close to being restored?

Yes, I could tell because I no longer wanted my marriage restored. It happened when he sent me a message wishing me a Happy Mother's Day. I hadn't been answering his texts, but I could tell my HH wanted me to reply. So I answered it as gently as I had learned in my lessons. Then he asked me if we could just talk, and the next day he returned home. It was all so sudden, I didn't expect anything, really. And also just as Erin says will happen, earlier in that same week the trials kept increasing, I seriously thought I might as well give up, another sign you're close.

So, please, dear bride, stand firm and watch God give you the restoration He promised. Trust me, the enemy will do anything and everything to steal your miracle. I tried fighting against myself early in my journey, because I wanted to call him and say I was going to file for divorce, give into my emotions. But I instead started to praise Him and suddenly God changed the situation.

Would you recommend any of our resources in particular that helped you, Maite?

Yes. How God can and will restore your marriage was essential. Each of the courses, the videos, the Word of God! The praise reports, restored testimonies and especially my 3x5 cards were extremely important.

Would you be interested in helping encourage other women, Maite?

Yes

Either way, Maite, what kind of encouragement would you like to leave women with, in conclusion?

Everyone told me to give up and thought I was crazy to continue. Several times I thought about giving up. But God was working for me without ever knowing. Pray, fast, praise and be quiet. These four things were very important to me. Pray for your enemies! Be patient, the urgency is usually the enemy's cunning ways. Your miracle will arrive, just as mine did. I didn't expect it, my marriage was dead, but by the blood of my Beloved Savior it was made alive. Glory God! Does your situation look impossible? Because "with God nothing is impossible." Luke 1:37. God bless you!

Chapter 11

Judie

"My son, do not despise the Lord's discipline,
and do not resent his rebuke,
because the Lord disciplines those he loves,
as a father the son he delights in."
— Proverbs 3:11-12

"Once I was Able to Let Go"

Judie, how did your Restoration Journey actually begin?

After a month and 9 days, my EH (earthly husband) came back. In all, he was gone 1 month and 22 days. We are both 23 years old and we have been married for just a year and a half. We always had problems because we are both young and attractive and so there has always been someone trying to make us betray each other, men and women, who do not give a damn about our marriage commitment. We constantly threw each other's past mistakes in each other's face during arguments just to hurt the other. We couldn't forgive.

One day we went to a party in a bar, a place I never liked to go to, when I realized just how far a Pharisee I'd become. I was ashamed, I thought I was more holy than the others and I thought they were so proud. At that party we had a lot of discussions and I made my EH feel ashamed in front of all his friends because he did things that I disliked. I was very quarrelsome. Everything had to be my way. I fought, I manipulated, I made everyone side with me. I was a total fool!! I was tearing down my house with my own hands. That day was the final straw in the sea of fights when my EH decided to leave me. But he didn't actually go and the fights continued until I told him to leave as I did many times before. When he still didn't he go, I packed my bags and said that I would leave if he didn't.

When he finally left, I didn't "let him go" instead, I would send him countless messages, and bombard him on every social network. That's when I discovered the OW (other woman). I was devastated, every photo I saw was like a slap in the face, a dagger in my heart. I finally realized that with my attitude, I was the one who had planted and watered all of this that I was now reaping.

Crying out to God, I found RMI in a comment after I posted prayer on a prayer app. After finding the RMI, I could feel God's presence in my life. I found out how much He cares about me and those I love. I found out that God made me go through this so that He could help me stop making mistakes. He reminded me of everything I ever asked Him, the times I told Him, "Father God, I don't want to make mistakes like these, help me"! When I read all the testimonies from couples who spent 12, 15, 20 years making mistakes in their marital lives, I knew I could change.

I started the course after reading the book How God can and will restore your marriage and soon I managed to "let go." Before coming here, my days were long, and there was no time to be with my beloved HH. Before coming here, working with people was a burden, I wanted to run away. Then it all changed, I wanted to run and scream to the world that He is my everything, telling them that before I cried with despair and was overwhelmed with sadness, and now I have contentment, peace and gratitude because my HH supplies everything!

How did God change your situation, Judie, as you sought Him wholeheartedly?

God continued showing me how wrong I was. How dirty I was a "whitewashed tomb" and how hypocritical I was, not listening to His warnings and not following His Word being ignorant to His principles.

At the beginning of my Restoration Journey I was devastated. My EH regularly came to our house to take care of the dog and after cleaning the kennel he returned to his mother's house where he stayed during that time. When he arrived I cried and made a point of showing him how sad I was, so of course he didn't talk to me much and soon left.

We arrived at this separation because I was contentious, quarrelsome, bitter, spiteful and we had been fighting for almost three months straight. Then, in one of the fights it became violent and hurt each other. I just didn't know how to control myself. Despite being a Christian and being in ministry, I could find no peace and our home reflected the turmoil.

Several times before our separation, I felt God urging me to kneel and pray and fast for my marriage but I never did. My EH was already distant, avoiding me and not wanting to be intimate with me. I searched everything of his, his cell phone, his Facebook and I even deleted several people from his social networks.

What principles, from God's Word (or through our resources), Judie, did the Lord teach you during this trial?

The principle of a gentle and quiet spirit, of pursuing my EH all the time, of having Him as first in everything in my life. Praying the Word, leaving social networks (note: I had tried to leave it several times and never managed to) and so many others!!!

What were the most difficult times that God helped you through, Judie?

When I discovered the OW and saw that my EH had erased all of our photos from the Social Networks. And when I was totally without light and water at home (before I'd let go and God turned my EH's heart to pay them). It was a lot of pressure for me and several times I wanted to give up and go back to my mother's house.

Judie, what was the "turning point" of your restoration?

The turning point of my restoration was when I was very content just to have my HH (Heavenly Husband) and I no longer cared so much about restoration but about encouraging others in a marriage crisis. It was then that my pastor called me and asked about my EH (I had shared my situation with many people before I knew the principle of keeping silent).

My EH began paying for my health plan (I am in the middle of treatment against an illness), he even paid for my phone plan and made purchases for me. Once I was able to let go, my EH approached me often. Even though he had already taken our dog, he always found an excuse to come to our house to see me once I had my HH. It was difficult not to fall back to the old me, but I kept Him first even after we began having an ongoing intimate relationship with my EH on a weekly basis.

Tell us HOW it happened, Judie? Did your husband just walk in the front door? Judie, did you suspect or could you tell you were close to being restored?

One afternoon when I got home there he was waiting for me. He stood up and held me and cried and asked if I still loved him. When I said Yes, he told me he regretted leaving, that he wanted to come home and so many other things that could only be GOD. God turned the heart of my EH to me once my heart was turned to Him!! it is incredible, HE is incredible! I know that God called me and called my EH for a great work in helping other couples. He came back completely different too. He now goes to church, and he reads the Word on his own! Glory to God Who transforms, changes, resurrects, Who finds what was once lost, Who takes what was over and gives it a New Beginning! I love You Lord! I can't contain the tears of joy! I used to know Him from hearing about Him but today I know who He is, He is mine and I am His.

Would you recommend any of our resources in particular that helped you, Judie?

The book how God can and will restore your marriage and A Wise Woman and your courses, all of them.

Would you be interested in helping encourage other women, Judie?

Yes

Either way, Judie, what kind of encouragement would you like to leave women with, in conclusion?

Do not give up! God is always in control!

"My son, do not despise the Lord's correction, And do not faint when you are rebuked by him; Because the Lord corrects what he loves, And whips anyone who receives as a son.

If you endure correction, God treats you like children; why, what son is there that the father does not correct?

But if you are without discipline, of which everyone is made a participant, then you are bastards, not children.

Besides, we had our parents according to the flesh, to correct us, and we revere them; will we not be subject much more to the Father of spirits, to live?

Because those, in fact, for a little while, corrected us as it seemed to them; but this, for our benefit, to be partakers of his holiness.

And, in fact, all correction, at present, does not seem to be one of joy, but of sadness, but then it produces a peaceful fruit of justice in those exercised by it.

Therefore, raise your tired hands again, and your knees disjointed, and make straight paths for your feet, so that what limps does not deviate entirely, but is healed." Hebrews 12: 5-13

Chapter 12

Elizabeth

"The iniquities of the wicked ensnare him,
and he is held fast in the cords of his sin."
—Proverbs 5:22

"I Won Him Without Saying a Word and My Behavior Drew Him"

Elizabeth, how did your Restoration Journey actually begin?

My husband and I got married when we were very young, I was 18 and he was 20. For both of us, we were each of our first boyfriend/girlfriend and we didn't know anything about a healthy marriage. I couldn't give myself to my husband, only after 1 month of marriage was there any intimacy between us. It was also something we did rarely, we were always very close friends, but mostly just friends, we didn't have an intimate relationship that is between husband and wife. I was in a lot of pain when we were intimate and that went on for almost 5 years until the fights over it became constant.

My husband was a pastor and our marriage looked to be perfect, but we both knew it wasn't. As a result of our infrequent intimacy, I struggled to get pregnant. When we were intimate, I cried because it felt like I was being raped. After a long time of trying, I got pregnant and everything was normal during pregnancy. For some reason our intimacy was no longer painful, it was, for awhile wonderful. We were very close and in love, but when I had our son, I went back to hurting like before.

The enemy took advantage of this and started putting OWs (other woman) in my husband's life. Thankfully he resisted them all. A short time later, my father passed away, and because he was lead pastor of our church, with his death, things got worse for us financially, because he always helped us when we needed it and my EH (earthly husband) was like his right-hand man. They confided in one another and with my father's passing, my EH became more and more distant from God because my father was an example, much used by God in healing, deliverance, and my EH mirrored him.

With his death, a lot changed, the church ministry decided to cut some expenses, and my EH became discouraged with the church, which led to him returning to college because the income of the church was not supporting us. He said he needed a profession and it was confirmed when his father (who was always distant and did not support him much about his life as a Christian) started to pay for college and became his best friend. The friendship grew the more he heard about his distancing himself from the church, and months later, my EH started to get involved with a "friend" in one of his classes.

When I found out, I sent a message to the OW, and she told me to work it out with my husband because he was on her side, she said. In my head, I needed to show her who his wife was and do the same with my EH. I fought, screamed, and that's when he said he was going to disappear because he didn't think there was much worth saving with us. That's when I got nervous and I changed my tactics, instead I apologized but instead of helping, he became more distant. I found out months later that he was having a relationship with the OW, and again, I did everything wrong. I threw his clothes on the floor, I kicked him out of our home, and I ran to tell my 3 sisters.

Not only did that silly stunt of mine cause my EH to move away from my family for good, but it brought him closer to the OW and solidified their relationship! My sisters bought a tracker and we put it on his car, we were sure they were together, and then proved it. After being confronted, he moved in with my mother-in-law, his mom, and after a month, I begged him to come back home. At first, I invented things to fill him with fear, but the Lord changed me and I stopped.

He did return home, but by that time the OW was already "the girlfriend" who I confronted regularly. I confronted him, said that I would tell her father that he was married and lived with me and that was it! For the first time, he came at me, he didn't hit me, but what I saw was not my husband. The hate wall was solidly built, we spoke only when necessary. He wanted a divorce,

Due to this I got horribly thin. I am tall and was already thin (120 lbs), but I lost another 30 lbs in about 2 or 3 months. I was nothing but skin and bones, and my face was downcast. Everyone who looked at me, I could see people's pity, I was a horrible mess.

We didn't sleep together anymore and we didn't have any intimacy. Now I was the one who wanted it and he wasn't interested in me. He left and came back when he wanted to, and when he was there, we fought, argued, I questioned him, each caused even more distance than before.

As if it wasn't already horrible, he started to go to a new church and he'd take the OW, and I heard she even "converted" and again I confronted him!

After a year of doing everything wrong and having nightmares almost every night, I said a sincere prayer to the Lord, I asked Him to tell me what His will was for me, if it was the restoration for my marriage, then I would have a happy dream and if not, I knew He was saying it was over.

That night, when I slept, I dreamed of my late father. Our family was all together and God had allowed him to visit us, my EH, my brothers-in-law, my mother, sisters and nephews—we were all together, smiling happily for my father's visit. I woke up smiling and the Lord reminded me of my prayer. After being able to eat breakfast for the first time in a long time, I went on the internet and started researching restored marriages, when I found on a blog the link to download the book How God Can and Will Restore Your Marriage. I downloaded it to my cell phone, and started reading, and realized how much I was doing wrong. Through the book, I got to know the website HopeAtLast.com and read with tears streaming down my face that it was my "Divine Appointment." I filled out the questionnaire and started the courses that morning.

During these last few months, I always asked the Lord for confirmation of His will for our family, and He speaks to me in verses and once more gave me dreams about EH. In one of the dreams we were in another state and I was the women's minister in that church, we were there for me to share our testimony.

I started to apply the principles of the book, some were easy, others felt like they were too difficult for me to achieve but I just kept trusting Him.

How did God change your situation, Elizabeth, as you sought Him wholeheartedly?

As soon as I started to surrender to the Lord, He began to transform me! I asked my EH for forgiveness for everything I did, I organized a little room (that used to be a mess) to be my spiritual war room. The Lord helped me to let go of my EH and let go of the church. I put a lock on my mouth, and each time I felt like asking or talking I spoke to Him instead. If my EH went out somewhere, I ran into my little room, told everything to Him. Then I searched, searched, searched, and asked Him for promises. I begged my Lord to be my Husband, to be my Love, my Everything, to be the First, and He did! Sometimes I fell and missed the mark but He lifted me up and comforted me. It was not easy, I believe that if I had not been so foolish, my marriage would have been restored more than a year ago, that first year that I went wrong and got every bit of worldly advice running rampant in the church!

But I didn't get tired of my journey, I loved to seek God, and what a relief to let the church go and begin to develop a true relationship with the Lord that I never had! I stopped snooping because I no longer cared what His plan was and instead I just trusted Him. I asked my sisters for forgiveness for having talked about my situation with them, I cried just for my Lord when I remembered how I'd been. I made Him my Everything, my Friend, Companion, Confidant, Counselor, and when I had no strength, I just cried in the lap of my Heavenly Father.

He came, always came, and was with me during "our" journey. He did so many small and big miracles in my life, there were so many that made me fall in love more and more with who He is. My son also started to fall in love with the Lord, he missed his father, and the Lord was making up for it when I shared how He was my HH and so that meant He was his Heavenly Father. This changed my son so much and I no longer worried about him.

Things began to change in the middle of last year when my husband started coming to me for intimacy. At first, I thought it was a bit strange since it was almost two years since we'd been intimate, but I saw that it was the hand of the Lord. He said he loved me again, and he wanted to fix his life. The hate wall fell brick by brick and I watched the Lord's heart for our family change everything!

Then, in January, I went on vacation, and he didn't go, because I went with my family. When I left, he told me to have some fun, and every day he called me. My mother-in-law later told me that he was impatient, counting the days until I was coming home because missing us so much. The Lord was working on every detail.

What principles, from God's Word (or through our resources), Elizabeth, did the Lord teach you during this trial?

Winning without words was paramount, not snooping too as it hurts us more than anything. Do not fall into the temptation of trying to tweak things about your EH, the enemy always prepares something bad for us to see and then takes us down! Instead, relish in your new relationship with your HH— take everything to the Lord, talk only with Him. Just let it go, how difficult it was to live with my EH, and many times I couldn't, but when I did give up trying and instead trusted, I would fall in love with Him.

What were the most difficult times that God helped you through, Elizabeth?

Wow, God knows how many hard hours we had together! All in all, it was two and a half years of journey and from the beginning until we were restored. The hardest had to be seeing the EH in photos with OW, seeing on social networks him showing society his relationship with her even while living with me, (until I came here, I had Facebook, Instagram, but just as soon as I read the course to delete social networks, I didn't think twice!) to know about their different trips and seeing their vacations together! To see my 6-year-old son say that he missed his father because even living together sometimes my son did not see him (because he left early and when he returned we were already asleep).

Knowing that my name was not in his cell phone contacts so that his picture with OW on Whatsapp would not appear to me (later understanding that this was His way of protecting me), the various bad news he told me, having seen in a college document that he was "going through a divorce" that thankfully never was true. When my father-in-law and mother-in-law went to meet the OW and his family welcomed her, even though they knew he was living with me. All of this hurt a lot, when I discovered it and lived through these things back when I didn't have an intimate relationship with the Lord yet. Finally, my father-in-law rented and furnished an apartment for the EH to meet with OW and she believed he was living there alone when he was living with me and our son.

Hearing from EH that he couldn't be my husband again because he didn't love me anymore and that he didn't see us married anymore. That he would give a settlement to me and our son if I'd just go away.

Elizabeth, what was the "turning point" of your restoration?

It was certainly when my focus became my Lord, I no longer prayed for the restoration of my marriage, but I focused on my restoration with the Lord. I wanted to be His bride and He made me want Him more and more. I cried out to Him for my husband's deliverance, but I didn't pray like a wife crying out for a husband, but I prayed for his life, that he might be restored to the Lord.

I turned my focus away from my problems and started looking on the internet for people who needed help with their marriages. I started writing down names and praying for them, and for those who posted an email, I sent an email with the link to the HopeAtLast.com website and chapter 1 of the book How God Can and Will Restore Your Marriage.

More and more He began to turn the heart of EH for our family. Then he asked for prayer because he wanted to get out of the life he was living, he recognized the enemy's stronghold on him. "His own iniquities will capture the wicked, and he will be held with the cords of his sin." Proverbs 5:22. Then he told me that I was his best friend and he only trusted me! I prayed to God for the Lord's love shining through me, drawing my EH to Him. Whenever my EH's family or friends saw me somewhere, they told my EH how beautiful I was. It had been months since I had let go of going to church and he started asking me to go and take our son. I cried to the Lord saying I didn't want this, I wanted him to take us, as a family, but I submitted to EH. I read the children's Bible to my son every day. My son told his father and his father was excited and remembered when he used to say that by the age of 5 our son would already be preaching in the church.

In the end, my EH started to go to church and take us about 3 or 4 months after our restoration.

Tell us HOW it happened, Elizabeth? Did your husband just walk in the front door? Elizabeth, did you suspect or could you tell you were close to being restored?

After about 10 months of finding RMI and the Lord helping me to improve to the point that my EH started saying that he wanted his family back. All in all, he broke up with OW but always went back, more than 10 times he told me they were no more, but everything was still the same. I started to pray the prayers in the RYM book and fasted that he would be freed from the cords of sin, "His own iniquities will capture the wicked, and he will be held with the cords of his sin." Proverbs 5:22 but when I realized that he was with her, it hurt me so much, that I gave up and told the Lord only HE could do it. THAT'S when it happened. When the battle is the Lord's, the victory is ours! "The LORD saves not with sword and spear. For the battle is the LORD's, and He will give you victory into your hand." 1 Samuel 17:47

He prayed that the prison would be opened and he would be free (Isaiah 58:6) that his legs, arms and eyes would be untied (Acts 12:7) and he could be resurrected for the Lord. (John 11:43)

I found out it finally happened when I was at my mother's, and he called me and said he was at church and was going to talk to the pastor because he wanted to come back. He wanted our family, he wanted me as his wife. He wanted to be free from the sinful life he was caught in. I almost didn't even believe it— I was so stunned.

After the service, we went to the pastor's house and he asked me for forgiveness, we talked and the pastor prayed for us.

After 2 weeks, at the supper service, the pastor called him forward, and he asked the church for forgiveness and said that "I won him without saying a word" and that my behavior drew him and he realized he wanted his life back! He also said that seeing our boy so thirsty and interested in the Lord made him see that he had already wasted too much time, that he wanted our family to be used by God.

After a few days, he took us to the movies (which we hadn't done in two and a half years) and booked a trip for 2 weeks for our family honeymoon. There will be four of Us: the Lord, EH, me, and our son!

My Lord, You are perfect. It was GOD who did it, it was You, Lord, who changed me. All honor and glory go to You.

Everything is not yet the way I imagined, but that's good news, isn't it? It keeps me focusing on being HIS bride rather than my EH's wife. My Lord remains in control, and I believe that our ministry will be resurrected to the glory of the Lord. My EH will become the spiritual leader of our home again and long to devote his life to ministry.

I pray that He will do what He's done for me to more and more of you, so that the Lord may be the first in your life and that you will feel that your HH loves you more than you could imagine and that God will restore you to Him. I pray that the Lord, my Beautiful and beloved Heavenly Husband, will make your EH the husband and father that God created him to be.

I praise You, Lord, for You are faithful and do not fail. I love You for who You are.

Would you recommend any of our resources in particular that helped you, Elizabeth?

Of course, starting with the book How God Can and Will Restore Your Marriage which was the first I found that gave me hope. Even to this day I read and reread portions of it with my HH (Heavenly Husband) in mind. Also the Wise Woman, both your devotionals, reading the praise reports, and without a doubt, your courses. Reading the lessons and the book brings comfort but journaling is what changes you. Everything you have is inspired by our Beloved, the way He wants it to be, glory to God for the life of Erin, and for RMI! Where would we be if He hadn't used you?

Would you be interested in helping encourage other women, Elizabeth?

Certainly, since before the journey, a phrase called my attention, it was like "the place where you were hurt, will be the place that God will use you most to help heal others"... today I understand where He wants to use me.

Either way, Elizabeth, what kind of encouragement would you like to leave women with, in conclusion?

My sister, sometimes looked for testimonies, someone who had a journey like mine, with EH living at home, because it seemed impossible to be able to let go. But the Lord showed me that He was with me, and all things He set up for our GOOD, (Romans 8:28). He assured me that because my journey was different, He was writing a testimony so my restoration was even more assured because it wasn't like anyone else's! This helped me at times when I doubted. I hope it will help you too.

We need to accept His will and know that what He promised, it will be fulfilled by Him. He cannot lie, (Hebrew 6:18) He does not fail or abandon us (Hebrews 13:5), His eyes are on us all the time. He always has the best for us! I praise him because it was necessary for me to go through all this, I thank Him for using this desert for my growth. Today I know Him and I walk with HIM, He is Everything I want and need.

Give your life and family to Him, you will not regret it. He will honor you, seek answers to your questions in His Word, He answers, He never lets us down. Fall in love with Him, travel this journey pain-free, and believe that You and your house will serve the Lord. He's everything we need.

Chapter 13

Dona

"A gentle answer turns away wrath,
But a harsh word stirs up anger."
—Proverbs 15:1

"EH Introduced Me to the OW. I Smiled and Said, "Hello, It's Nice to Meet You"

Dona, how did your Restoration Journey actually begin?

During our seven years of marriage, my husband had left two times. We didn't fight but we always argued. Most of the time because things don't go as I would like. I was a contentious, quarrelsome woman, did not honor my husband and humiliated him in front of my family. Being submissive? That word always left me feeling discouraged and trapped. When I started college I heard that as women we should say everything we thought and "set out to fight for what we wanted" and that means discussing everything and making sure you win, so you'd get what you wanted.

Just to give you an idea, I thought I could act in the most obnoxious way and I would still be admired and cherished. I have been a Christian since I was young and my dream was always to raise a family and be married forever. I loved the word "marriage" but didn't have a clue what would keep a marriage strong and happy.

Incredibly I saw myself as a humble person and I was sure that I was looking for God in the right way. What a hypocrite I was. I didn't beat my chest in public to say what I did but I thought everything everyone else did was wrong according to God's principles.

My husband always told me to listen to him, to say only what I needed to say, not to talk to everyone about our intimacy (don't ever do that). But it seems that I could not understand what was missing and besides,

I always opposed anything he said, I did not support him in most conversations we had.

During the period just before this, I had always had a great thirst for God and had decided that I no longer wanted a meaningless life. I wanted something different. I wanted to live being guided by God just as the prophets lived, so I started looking for it by reading the Word, praying, and looking for books in that sense to become more spiritual.

One day while surfing the internet, I found the book "the power of the praying wife" and immersed myself in prayer for my husband, which I did very superficially. After three weeks of prayer and fasting, my husband said to me after an argument, "I'm going to take a trip to rethink our marriage. We simply don't work as a married couple, please respect me."

Let me explain that prior to this he had already proposed that I quit my job to take better care of our children and finish school, but I decided not to obey him and that I was the only one who could hear from God. I was sure he was going to come back changed, but instead, when he came back from the trip he told me that he was leaving because we were no longer working as a married couple. He also told me he had met someone else and had not loved me for some time. That he'd tried to make it right (by what he had earlier proposed) and that he was still with me due to the children but that he would not even stay for them now. I was impossible to live with.

How did God change your situation, Dona, as you sought Him wholeheartedly?

That was the end for me. Desperation came over me so the only way I knew was to go to God in prayer and that's what I did and asked Him to guide me to find something to follow. Because I believed that nothing is impossible for God I just needed it to be true, I needed to live what was impossible. God guided me through the Internet to find the RMI website. When I started to read the testimonies of restored marriages on the website, I was filled with hope, so I downloaded the book How God can and will restore your marriage and I read it in three days, then read it again, and then again.

From then on, I was able to see how I acted so horribly and how my prideful attitude made my husband not feel supported. It was his dream to have a united family (because he grew up with a separate father and mother so he always wanted that: a wife, children always together). What I gave him was nothing but deep frustration. At first, I couldn't forgive myself for it. I loved him but I had made him suffer a lot.

But God is so wonderful; He made me see how silly I was, how contentious, quarrelsome, and hypocritical. He broke me and reshaped me and changed me and has been changing me just the way He wants me to be!

What principles, from God's Word (or through our resources), Dona, did the Lord teach you during this trial?

Reading the book God gave me strength and I started to apply all the principles that I didn't know and never heard. I'm still shocked how no one in the church, no retreat, no Bible studies ever taught me the truth on marriage. It's shocking.

So, without knowing the truth, first, God had to each me to purify myself and He broke my heart. Then I started to apply the principles of "letting go" and getting out of his way. I learned to make my God my first in everything and I didn't run to the phone anymore as I did in each crisis. When that happened God turned my husband's heart back to me. But first I needed to be tested.

At his brother's wedding where my son was a ring bearer, he took OW and introduced me to her. I smiled and said, "Hello, it's nice to meet you." I was "gentle and quiet" winning without words. At the end of the wedding, my husband took me home, and on the way, he said to me "Congratulations, you managed to get rid of another one of my dates." I replied that I was sorry, that I hadn't meant to say anything to mess things up. He said he knew it wasn't my fault, but the fact that he had his wedding ring on is what really made her break up with him. (During our separation he never stopped using your wedding ring.)

What were the most difficult times that God helped you through, Dona?

The most difficult moments were at the beginning when I still did not feel the peace that surpasses all understanding. That didn't happen until I did the courses Finding and then Living the Abundant Life.

The other difficult time was when I worked and didn't come home until dawn, then being present for my kids when they'd wake up. I prayed and asked God to change that situation and He did! Without telling anyone, my graveyard shift was changed to days. Now since my restoration I am a stay at home mom!

Dona, what was the "turning point" of your restoration?

The turning point was when he introduced me to OW and I didn't say anything unkind or create a scene in front of his family. I never asked him about anything that was happening or asked anyone else about it. This spoke volumes to my EH and our family and friends, but it was God who saw and had favor on me.

Tell us HOW it happened, Dona? Did your husband just walk in the front door? Dona, did you suspect or could you tell you were close to being restored?

In fact, after that wedding, he began sleeping at home every other night. He did trip up and was with the OW, but again, I said nothing even though he knew I knew. He stayed away two nights and a day. Then he was home for good, physically, and emotionally. Being home and with the OW gone for good, he became more relaxed every day.

He didn't say anything, he just came back. I also didn't ask any questions about anything that happened. Now I am trusting God to make my EH the spiritual leader of our home and I believe it is close. I let my church go so I have made room for him and will leave the details to God

Would you recommend any of our resources in particular that helped you, Dona?

I recommend all RMI materials starting with the Bible that is our foundation, after the book how God can and will restore your marriage, a wise woman, the encourager, the testimonies of restored marriages, and the lessons of the courses, all of them.

Would you be interested in helping encourage other women, Dona?

Yes, I already encourage other women. I share the HopeAtLast.com site because God told us to share the good news. We need to share with women who are suffering and need hope.

Either way, Dona, what kind of encouragement would you like to leave women with, in conclusion?

Never give up on seeking restoration for your lives, families, marriages and always put our God first in everything in your lives because He is who will turn the heart where He wants: towards you or away from you. Even though you may not see any evidence that things are changing, you have to know that God is at work and restoration is moving towards you.

Chapter 14

Meliza

"For as many as the promises of God are,
in Him they are yes; therefore through Him
also is our Amen to the glory of God through us."
—2 Corinthians 1:20

"EH was Transferred and I Refused to Go with Him"

Meliza, how did your Restoration Journey actually begin?

I want to thank my HH (Heavenly Husband) who allowed me to go through this desert and show me how much I was wandering due to being religious. I was always a very contentious woman, everything had to be my way and without realizing it I hurt my husband. Looking back I see how foolish it was as I did not build my house on the Rock. It made my husband feel rejected in all aspects, including our intimacy. I was so foolish when my EH (earthly husband) was transferred from where we lived and I refused to go with him because I complained I would have to live in a small town and leave my house. We stayed apart for 2 years, living in separate houses.

This physical distance between my husband from me caused me to also emotionally distance myself from him too because I wanted him to come to know the Lord, playing a junior holy spirit. Instead of seeking the Lord for himself, my husband became aggressive, distant, sad and one day when he came to our vacation home from work, he said that he didn't know what he felt for me anymore, that we were very different, and that it was better for each of us to go his/her own way. I finally realized that things were not so good, that my marriage was falling apart. I panicked and asked my husband for just a bit more time, I asked him to try to change and I would try to change too. Then I asked him to take me back with him where he worked, but he said he didn't want that anymore. I suspected that he had an OW, but he always denied it.

So we remained in this situation for another 8 months, continued with many fights, a lot of suffering for both of us, and soon the wear and tear began to get to us both. Then one day I was looking for evidence of an OW (other woman) and I found some pictures when I logged into his email account. I said many terrible things to him, thinking he would ask me for forgiveness. To my disappointment and shock, he confessed that he really had an OW, that he loved her, that he didn't love me anymore, that he had no intention of staying in our marriage, and moved out of the house completely.

How did God change your situation, Meliza, as you sought Him wholeheartedly?

At the height of my pain, now entirely alone, I began to search for restored marriage testimonies on YouTube and a comment caught my attention. It said God CAN restore your marriage, He restored mine! I contacted this sister who posted it and she directed me to the website HopeAtLast.com and I just knew it was my Divine Appointment. I started reading the book How God can and will restore your marriage when the scales fell from my eyes.

It happened in an instant God spoke to me! I could see how far I was from His principles even though I was attending church and how I had been ruthless towards my husband. I began to seek God with all my heart, repenting of all my sins and surrendering all my pain and disappointments to Him. I needed to change, I could not continue to be contentious, aggressive, agitated. God said He restores marriages, but I imagined it would take too long so I concentrated on getting myself right with my Heavenly Beloved and left any restoration to Him.

What principles, from God's Word (or through our resources), Meliza, did the Lord teach you during this trial?

The principle of letting go, of not getting in the way of my husband, not wanting to know about his life and OW. The principle of knowing how to be quiet, which was hard because I always had something to say to justify myself but I learned to listen, to remain gentle, and respond quietly to anything he said. The principle of having lovable and sweet lips, to meditate on the Word of God and pray the Bible verses as His promises to me.

What were the most difficult times that God helped you through, Meliza?

During the many hours of solitude, you know when the pain was so strong? I would put on a hymn and cry like a child and get up into the lap of my Heavenly Father. Also, something very difficult was dealing with the shame. Nobody likes to be betrayed and I was very ashamed of my broken marriage. It was difficult to hear certain comments from family and friends, but I held on to God's promises and trusted in His actions, knowing He would complete what He began.

Meliza, what was the "turning point" of your restoration?

The turning point was when I knew I was fine. I had no anxiety anymore, in fact, I was already loving my life with my Heavenly Beloved. I came to the point of not wanting my marriage restored but telling my HH "God's will be done." My husband started to notice that I was happy—much different from the woman he left and then he started looking for me, to talk and then looking for me to be intimate. I was always kind to him and not once did I pursue him. After we were intimate, I just up and left (after telling my HH how much it hurt to be so close and then to be walked out on). That shocked my EH and later he said it was a wake-up call and he began to worry he'd lost me.

Tell us HOW it happened, Meliza? Did your husband just walk in the front door? Meliza, did you suspect or could you tell you were close to being restored?

One day he started looking for me, saying he couldn't sleep, that he thought about us a lot. A day or two later he called me and said that I wasn't supposed to think it was over for us, that there was a chance we could come back and be together again. I started to disconnect more and more, turning off my cell phone, not answering emails. I really just wanted to devote myself to spending time with my Heavenly Beloved. Meanwhile, God was turning my husband's heart toward me.

One day my husband sent a message saying that he loved me, that he wanted to come back, that he was done with OW. Then I said I was wanted to offer him unconditional love and forgiveness, that he was my husband and I wanted to live with him. However, he was still a little confused as he worked in another city. So he ended up spending 15 more days there. I confess that I was at first afraid he would give up, but then I remembered I wasn't interested in restoration anyway and got really happy! I turned my attention to seeking my Beloved and only spoke briefly to my husband if he was looking for me. Until he called me and said he was on his way, packed and driving to our house. He came back and the next week was transferred back to our city where he works now.

Would you recommend any of our resources in particular that helped you, Meliza?

Yes. I recommend all materials especially the book as God can and will restore your marriage. The courses, videos, encourager.

Would you be interested in helping encourage other women, Meliza?

Yes. I found help because someone posted hope on YouTube. I want to be able to help other women who go through this situation and hope that any of you reading this will post testimonies to give hope to the hopeless who are out there afraid and alone.

Either way, Meliza, what kind of encouragement would you like to leave women with, in conclusion?

My loved ones do not give up fighting for your family, for this is the will of God for you. Enjoy the journey of restoration and have more intimacies with the Lord if you let yourself be shaped by Him, trust in His word, rest your heart in Him because every promise that God made you He will fulfill and you will not be ashamed.

"For all of God's promises have been fulfilled in Him with a resounding "Yes!" And through Him, our "Amen" (which means "Yes") ascends to God for his glory." 2 Corinthians 1:20

Chapter 15

Arthur

"But examine everything; hold firmly to that which
is good, abstain from every form of evil."
— 1 Thessalonians 5:21-22

"She Loved Me and Forgave Me"

Arthur, how did your Restoration Journey actually begin?

It happened soon after I no longer prayed as when I met my wife and did not read the word anymore. The passion started to end after 2 years of marriage and the difficulties of living together were unbearable.

Physical aggression began to occur by both parties and disrespect became more and more constant. My wife left home for a few days 2 times.

In the last fight, where we attacked each other, she left and this time, took her things. The final step was she threw her ring out on the street. I was alone and crumbled.

How did God change your situation, Arthur, as you sought Him wholeheartedly?

First, He showed me that I was a long way from the standard He set. I was stubborn, greedy, anxious, had a hard heart, did not forgive, and was not dependent on GOD.

Reading the books mainly of A Wise Man, because it taught me to behave according to the will of God. How God will restore your marriage has given me "hope against hope." I was already thinking about abandoning my marriage restoration and looking for someone new.

But when I started to pray, God took things from the world out of my heart and brought "a peace that surpasses all understanding."

What principles, from God's Word (or through our resources), Arthur, did the Lord teach you during this trial?

Prayer, Fasting, Reading the Word, Do not go after the spouse, Do not speak ill of anyone, do not keep watching the spouse's life, give your tithe.

What were the most difficult times that the Lord helped you through, Arthur?

When I was in sexual and emotional abstinence. It was very difficult to let my wife go and abandon all sexual sin, in fact, I struggled with it every day until the end of my time in the desert. And another difficulty was when I was afraid that my wife would not come back and she'd find another man.

Arthur, what was the "turning point" of your restoration?

When my wife spoke to me on her own again. I did not speak to her for a month. The first signs were the favorable things and her status she posted.

God had also clearly spoken to me in the months before, and the best thing was that I hadn't even asked Him about it. I realized that my spiritual life with the Lord was getting better every day. I spent more time praying, the hours increased and I fasted almost every day.

Tell us HOW it happened, Arthur? Did your wife just walk in the front door? Arthur, did you suspect or could you tell you were close to being restored?

When my wife posted on the status of her cell phone that she loved me and forgave me.

Would you recommend any of our resources in particular that helped you, Arthur?

Yes, all books. The book how to deal with divorce, Facing Divorce, was very good because it has some excellent testimonies. A Wise Man and the Be Encouraged videos were encouraging and were sensational.

I took Courses 1-4 and just finished Rebuilding with Intelligence, Knowledge, Precious & Pleasant Wealth.

Would you be interested in helping encourage other men, Arthur?

YES

Either way, Arthur, what kind of encouragement would you like to leave men with, in conclusion?

That they must be delivered from all fear and anxiety at the feet of the Lord and your physical and emotional needs too. Stay away from every appearance of evil, such as friends, who lead you on paths that are contrary to God's will.

Stay away from other women because at this stage we are very vulnerable to any of them.

And search the Bible for the will of God who longs to restore your family.

Chapter 16

Alexandra

"He sent His word and healed them,
And saved them from their destruction."
—Psalm 107:20

"I Was Taken To A Psychiatric Hospital Where I Was Committed"

Alexandra, how did your Restoration Journey actually begin?

Since I started this course, just sensing I was close to being restored, I kept wondering how I could possibly write my testimony. I wondered if I would go into detail because remembering some things I thought would be too painful to even think about and much worse having to write it down for everyone to read. What would it be like to remember everything that happened? But one thing I knew for sure, that through it all He is here with me, by my side, holding my hands, keeping me steady as I write.

Let me start by stating that I was contentious, spiteful, proud, and an obnoxious self-righteous woman. What's worse is that I didn't realize it. I had no clue. When I met my EH (earthly husband) I was no longer attending church and very far away from God. But a short time later the Lord called me back and then I started to seek Him. I admit it was out of fear, but the Lord used it to show me I was missing His wonderful Love.

Even though I was going to church again, I was looking for Him there, not at home where I could find true intimacy with Him. As time passed and I let myself be carried away by the lures of the enemy and my heart turned away from the Lord, as I said above, I became a Pharisee. I read the Bible, prayed, cried, but all while tearing my house down with my hands... more accurately with my own tongue.

Dissatisfaction and ingratitude were what ignited me and fueled the destruction of my home and my family. And everything got worse after the birth of our first child, not that it's my son's fault at all! I went into postpartum depression and by foolishly seeking medical advice, I was given antidepressants and a psychologist who messed with my head and heart. It all got very bad. It was much worse as I began to become dependent on drugs and talking, talking, talking about my problems, blaming everyone, especially my husband. I was fat, my body was ugly. I blamed the lack of family support.

And because my heart was far from the Lord, even though I tried to put into practice what I had learned in the church who starved me spiritually, I got so angry I broke things at home, and one day my EH (earthly husband) couldn't take it anymore. I remember that a few days before (what I am about to say), I had woken up at dawn and cried out to God to do a miracle and save me, save my family. Well ... He heard my prayer, but like so many testimonies I read said, it was not at all the miracle I imagined. Today, of course, I see that it was the better way, His way, the only way I'd be who I am now.

After the last straw, which was a fight in which I broke things at home and I threatened to kill myself. My EH (earthly husband) had to run across the street to beg for help from a few of our neighbors. Then he left and went to a crisis center here in the city (all this without me knowing) to see if he could forcibly commit me. Looking back, I still feel terrified and why I need His help sharing this. Yet, throughout the entire ordeal, His hand was there in it all. He was there and at all times He never left me alone!

The day after my EH sought to find out about having me committed, I was more furious than before and in a rage. My EH was with our 6-month-old son who he'd taken to the park when I heard a knock at the door. Without much explanation, I was taken to a psychiatric hospital where I was committed. Yes, I was there for 7 days against my will, and today I can clearly see that the Lord gave me the grace to endure what happened there and peace that can surpass all understanding! I will give Him Glory forever for that!

The first night I refused to sleep or eat. I fasted, prayed, and asked God to get me out of there and save my marriage! But still, I had such horrible hate in my heart for what my EH had done, for doing this to me and instead of talking to me or warning me, so it took a long time for God to open my eyes so that I could see the good that He was planning for us, for me and to be open to forgive him.

In all, I stayed for 3 months, and the most painful was I had no contact with our son. Yes, my baby grew up without me being by his side, and even began to walk without me seeing it. BUT the Lord needed this to happen in order for me to destroy all my idols and wipe from my lips the names of the Baals! My main idol was me! Everything was about me. I needed to be taken to the desert so that He could speak to my heart and that is what makes me rejoice in happiness!!!

My EH and our children were also my idols, but the Lord's supernatural love abounded over all sin!!! Honor and Glory to Him, my King, and my God, my Husband, my Lover!!!

After some time, they released me into the care of another recovery center and where I had a tiny bit more freedom. I could go out and everything, but I still wasn't allowed to see my son. The first time I saw him was on his first birthday. The visit was supervised and I wasn't able to hold or touch him. He didn't know me, so I frightened him. As this meeting went well, I was given more visits with him, always with supervision. Dear reader, I'm only telling you these details so you know that a situation that seemed so impossible, so horribly tragic, is still not impossible with God. Our GOD makes the impossible completely possible!

What happened to me, whatever has happened to you, only happens because He wants to save not only you—but your family too! So believe in His love!!!

During this period, my contact with my EH was limited to just a few text messages, he did not answer my calls, which looking back I'm so thankful for. I wasn't ready, I hadn't fully forgiven, so I would (as Erin has said) verbally vomit my pain on him. I didn't speak to him (other than texts) for a full year because of where we live. In our country, there is a one year process to grant a divorce with no contact. Even though I hated him, I didn't want a divorce. But praise be to God, that was a wonderful lesson that the Lord made me learn by having to face divorce. Praise Him for His unfathomable mercy!!!

Well, it was this season of my desert when I was given the book How God Can and Will Restore Your Marriage—right after I asked Him for a "manual on what to do" something like "step by step."

How did God change your situation, Alexandra, as you sought Him wholeheartedly?

The Lord used several people and situations to isolate me from my family and my EH's family, everyone. It truly was a desert, but it was in that same desert that He gave me streams of freshwaters, His Word, that began to wash me and heal me. "...Christ loved the church and gave Himself up for her, so that He might sanctify her, having cleansed her by the washing of water with the Word, that He might present to Himself the bride in all her glory, having no spot or wrinkle or any such thing; but that she would be holy and blameless and whole." Ephesians 5:25-27 I was broken enough to accept the truths that He wanted me to know through the book How God Can and Will Restore Your Marriage, and right after I asked Him for a manual on what to do, something like step by step, I was given A Wise Woman.

In the beginning, I only applied a few things to my life. I was quite irregular with the courses and principles, but then I decided to take responsibility and try to be submissive when I read that the lessons and that my journals should be done EVERY day. There is no greater therapy. As bad off as I was, I was becoming a new person daily.

I came to understand that all this had happened for the purpose of turning to me to Him and to His truth. "Then the Lord said to me, 'You have seen well, for I am watching over My Word to perform it.'" Jeremiah 1:12.

"For I am confident of this very thing, that He who began a good work in you will perfect it [until it is finally finished] [bringing it to full completion] until the day of Christ Jesus." Philippians 1:6 AMP

So I began first to turn to my God, my Heavenly Father because His great love attracted me. Next, I began to be thankful for my time in the desert, and there I was able to meet Him more and more. No, He didn't change my situation, but He used it to change me and heal my traumas, fears, frustrations, and insecurities. It was in this desert that He showed me what a Father's love is, a Father who supplies every need, Who dresses, feeds, protects, cares, listens, consoles, corrects, and disciplines His children with firmness and love.

"He sent His word and healed them, and delivered them from ALL their destructions." Psalm 107:20

"So shall My word be that goes forth from My mouth; It shall not return to Me void, but it shall accomplish what I please, And it shall prosper in the thing for which I sent it." Isaiah 55:11 NKJV

Oh, what a BLESSED DESERT - Oh my sweet Love, may all Glory be to You!!!

It was in that same desert where He showed me and also healed me from the stigmas of loving relationships that I had in the past, the fear of abandonment, rejection, and my need for manipulation. While journaling through each of the Abundant Life Courses, I discovered my HH "Heavenly Husband" who is sweet, the perfect Companion, Friend, Protector, Provider, and the most patient of all men. I met the Husband of my Dreams, while in the desert. My favorite thing I believe is how easy it is to talk to Him. To quote your book Erin "My beloved is mine, and I am His . . . When I found Him whom my soul loves; I held on to Him and would not let him go . . . For I am [indeed] lovesick" (Song of Solomon 3:2–4; 5:8).

Today I was even thinking and telling Him that most of the time I don't even know what to talk to my EH about because I've said it all to Him. With Him, I can open up and talk and say whatever without being judged and without worrying someone will show up and lock me away. My HH listens to me, understands me, and knows everything before I even utter a word and He always answers me, although many times I need to wait. But that's okay—He's always here, ALWAYS, always with me while I wait!!!

You are my Perfect Love!!!

What principles, from God's Word (or through our resources), Alexandra, did the Lord teach you during this trial?

Seek Him before anything else ... Have no other gods, but go to Him first, because He is your Creator and your Husband (whether you acknowledge Him or not)! And it is He who is above our husbands, even though our husbands do not know it or may not accept it!!! Run to Him before anything!!! And wait!!! Get out of your EH path. Don't try to stop whatever it is you think he's doing... even doing to you.

Close your mouth. Dear Brides, I know it's hard! But just shut up. That means in texts or talking to anyone. Being quiet is the miracle cure along with being washed in His Word. It's miraculous!!!

Letting go of the Potter's hands. And finally praising Him always and for everything!!! Not just the good but the bad as well.

What were the most difficult times that God helped you through, Alexandra?

The most difficult moments? As you probably have guessed there are just so many, so many I can't even remember right now, because He healed me so deeply that I don't even remember. Oh, I do remember something that I haven't mentioned yet. Something that was very difficult and that He helped me overcome, that I completely forgot until now. It was when I was living in the last step before my release. My EH "invited" me to come over to where she lived and to meet the OW (other woman).

I'm sure the enemy meant to use it to set me back to square one, for me to go into a rage, but my life was on the Rock, I was stable in Him. So when the rains came, I did not fall. When I walked through the flood, it did not overtake me. Instead, I was given an early release and began living alone on my own. Gradually He opened my heart to see the beauty of being with Him, in the company of Him only. Oh, my Love, YOU are my Husband, my Everything!!!

Alexandra, what was the "turning point" of your restoration?

The turning point is when I acted in faith and marched in through the middle of the Red Sea without knowing whether it would open up. And doing so without even understanding, but just trusting Him, trusting His will and His Perfect Plan. Love that never fails!!!

"Love never stops loving. It extends beyond the gift of prophecy, which eventually fades away. It is more enduring than tongues, which will one day fall silent. Love remains long after words of knowledge are forgotten." 1 Corinthians 13:8 TPT

Tell us HOW it happened, Alexandra? Did your husband just walk in the front door? Alexandra, did you suspect or could you tell you were close to being restored?

I am not sure how it all happened, I only know that God acted in a unique and surprising way. My EH contacted me, the Lord turning his heart (Proverbs 21:1) and got him to do everything. I just had to keep myself close to my Beloved and watch the Lord fight for me and my family. "Do not be afraid; be still, and see the deliverance of the Lord, who will do for you today." Exodus 14:13.

I can only say that He was faithful to fulfill His Word when He said:

"The things that the eye did not see, and the ear did not hear, and did not go up into man's heart, are the things that God has prepared for those who love him." 1 Corinthians 2: 9 ACF.

"Believe in the Lord Jesus and you and your house will be saved." Acts 16:3.

I never thought I'd be a mother, a homemaker, or a wife again, but I am all those things. I'm very close to my son and my other children don't seem to remember me ever being gone. Only the God of the impossible could do that!

Would you recommend any of our resources in particular that helped you, Alexandra?

Of course, I recommend the book How God Can and Will Restore Your Marriage and the Courses, taking the Courses is very important! You must journal, you must! Read the Word and obey the principles in each of the books that are based on the Word!!! God used Erin Thiele to put everything in a book and then offer the courses through the generosity of the RMI partners. Trust me that nothing can change you like these resources and God's Word.

Would you be interested in helping encourage other women, Alexandra?

Yes! Yes!!! I hope my testimony will help encourage other women and give them hope.

Either way, Alexandra, what kind of encouragement would you like to leave women with, in conclusion?

There are so many ways I'd love to encourage you. First, try to open your eyes to see that all that is happening is His Love for you and your family, He is GOOD! HE IS GOOD! And no matter how bad, this situation will not kill you!

Turn to God, your Heavenly Father, and see that He makes sure you will continue being faithful to Him after your marriage is restored. Ask yourself: And after the children have grown up? After I get old? After I die? And then? And then?

Your marriage here on earth ends one day, but your marriage with the Lord is forever!!!

Work with the Lord keeping your family's salvation first in your heart. So many of my family have seen my transformation and have believed in Him because of it. You don't have to say anything to them, let the Lord do it by how you exhibit a gentle and quiet spirit, submissive to your EH.

Trust Him. He is God and not a man!

Glory, Glory, Glory to Him from now on through Eternity!!!

Chapter 17

Jennifer

"Then you will know the truth,
and the truth will set you free."
—John 8:32

"My Ex Is Now My Husband and We Are So Happy"

Jennifer, how did your Restoration Journey actually begin?

Praise, You, My Beloved for loving me so much and teaching me what it means to love and be loved!

I was married 10 years to another man, had a daughter, and was a fool. I let anger and spite take over my heart and we parted, I got divorced and went to live my life. I should mention I had several other boyfriends.

About 4 years later, I met someone much younger than me, we got involved and soon we were living together. We went through many things together and so each of the readers understands the power of God in my life I will share just a bit more. He was a young man, full of dreams and who came from a life full of problems, involved with drugs and the pregnancy of a girl in his teens when I met him. He was about to be a father but even though the age difference was no obstacle, since I was both working and in college, with him at home, living the life of a young man, soon it started to unravel.

Being older and having been married, needless to say, I was very arrogant. I humiliated him a lot, especially when I uncovered he'd been unfaithful to me. Because he was a child, I foolishly thought I was in control of the situation. It only got worse, I couldn't stand it and kicked him out of my house. Then the unthinkable happened, a few months after he left and I wanted to be rid of him, I found out I was pregnant. When I told him he could come back, he didn't want to come back saying he was with a girl his age and was happy. That's when it hit me and I realized I had done everything wrong in my first marriage.

Several times this guy came back only to leave when I kicked him out again and again. During this period our daughter was born. Alone I cried in utter despair!

How did God change your situation, Jennifer, as you sought Him wholeheartedly?

One day someone saw my despair and texted me the link to Hopeatlast. The second I arrived at your site I explored and devoured everything I could, I ordered the book How God can and will restore your marriage, PRAISE GOD and hallelujah! Finally the truth I was seeking. That book and this ministry changed my life, praise be to God. I had already been an evangelical believer (I know it's hard to believe). I was even baptized but I had never learned or been taught the ways of the Lord. I always had God in my heart, I prayed, was part of a prayer chain, but nothing gave me a relationship with Him. The fruits of my life were parties, dancing, and drinking, but no one said a thing or pointed me in the right direction to the truth, to Him!

From the moment I started taking the courses, on that very first day, I discovered that I was a foolish, contentious, quarrelsome woman and decided to give my life to God, hallelujah. I wanted to change, I wanted to be reconciled with God but didn't know how. Since that day I have spent incredible moments with My Beloved in the sweetest times of intimacy as He cleansed my soul.

What principles, from God's Word (or through our resources), Jennifer, did the Lord teach you during this trial?

The Lord taught me that I needed to love Him first, to love no one else more than I loved Him. Next, to seek Him first, not to ask anyone for help. He taught me to read the Bible, to take pleasure in His law, desiring to do His will, and He continues teaching me every day. I learned, did not need to try to memorize, the teachings of God, the verses that meant the most to me that I quickly marked in my bible, and then made the 3x5 cards to carry and read all day long. It's amazing how my thoughts and decisions are based on the Word of the Lord.

What were the most difficult times that God helped you through, Jennifer?

There were several times I cried at the feet of My Beloved, but when I found out that my daughter's father was dating and went on Facebook to see the woman's profile, I cried a lot that night, but that's when the Lord spoke to me about my first marriage and I thought of my ex. I'd heard he had never remarried but I had no idea where he was and was sure he'd want nothing to do with me.

Jennifer, what was the "turning point" of your restoration?

From the beginning, I tried to apply the principle of letting go, but it was not easy, I was still chasing my boyfriend, even though I didn't want to. But as soon as the Lord opened my eyes, and began to turn my heart toward my ex-husband, it was easy to let go.

So I sought God to restore my first marriage. I wasn't sure if He wanted to but I knew that nothing was impossible with Him. I asked Him if He wanted to restore my relationship with my daughter's father, I was open to His plan. I just needed to focus on my relationship with Him and let things happen.

Tell us HOW it happened, Jennifer? Did your husband just walk in the front door? Jennifer, did you suspect or could you tell you were close to being restored?

One day while I was singing one love song over and over to Him, I got a text from someone I didn't recognize. It was from my ex! He asked if we could meet, I said yes, and the next day I met him at our favorite burger place. My heart was beating so fast I felt like I would faint, but then I heard the Lord whisper, "Just trust Me" and then a flood of verses began pouring over my mind and settling my heart.

It all seemed so impossible. I always felt a certainty that nothing was impossible, but this?! My testimony isn't like any of the other testimonies I've read, none looked like mine. But God spoke to my heart all the time so I didn't give up and trusted Him.

My ex is now my husband and we are so happy. We are weathering the storms of life together as a family. Even though I didn't think it possible for my life to work out, it has. I wasn't the only one with a child, my husband fathered a child, a daughter, who is the same age as my daughter. We co-parent but it's always challenging to navigate how to deal with one issue after another springing up but it's working for our good because it means staying in His Word and living each of His principles.

Would you recommend any of our resources in particular that helped you, Jennifer?

YES, all the RMI materials, read them all, seek God first, but devour everything, read the bible, the books, take the courses, read the entire page on every one of their sites, everything. They are all based on the truth in God's Word. "You will know the truth and the truth will set you free!!" Just as He set me free!! Hallelujah!!

Would you be interested in helping encourage other women, Jennifer?

Yes of course.

Either way, Jennifer, what kind of encouragement would you like to leave women with, in conclusion?

How can I possibly begin? First, do not give up on pursuing His plan for your life! In my case, it seemed so utterly impossible. I never imagined that My Beloved was going to give me back my former husband or another daughter to love and mother as my own.

Even though it seems unbearable, look to God, love Him like a Lover, talk to Him, hold on to Him tightly, and don't ever let go. God will give you victory. I praise God for everything. If it weren't for Him in my life, I would still be nothing, living a life of sin and despair. I praise GOD for the life of Erin, for her family, and all the missionaries who make this site work.

Chapter 18

Jasmine

"If you listen carefully to the LORD your God
and do what is right in his eyes, if you pay attention
to his commands and keep all his decrees,
I will not bring on you any of the diseases
I brought on the Egyptians,
for I am the LORD, who heals you."
—Exodus 15:26

"In Therapy for 10 Years, Only God could Heal Me"

Jasmine, how did your Restoration Journey actually begin?

It was clear to everyone that our marriage was not going well. My EH (earthly husband) started doing extra work and he didn't spend much time at home anymore, he didn't go out with me and his daughters anymore. We spent any time we had together fighting and to make everything much worse, I took all the problems with my EH to my analyst (I had been in therapy for 10 years and didn't know only God could heal me). Then, one day my EH told me that he wanted to separate. My world fell apart. Despite all of our problems, I had never thought about separating and I didn't want to, it also never crossed my mind that my EH would one day ask for a separation.

After I went to another appointment with my analyst, I decided to have a conversation with my EH and confront him about it as my therapist suggested. During the conversation, he told me that he wanted to take a break and would go to his parents' house. He was so desperate to be rid of me, he went that same day, without taking anything, only the clothes on his back. And I collapsed. I felt like I had fallen into a bottomless chasm with no light and no way out.

How did God change your situation, Jasmine, as you sought Him wholeheartedly?

I have always had faith in God and have always sought Him out in the difficult moments of my life, but I never had a true relationship with Him. That was about to change. A few days before my EH left home, I opened a Bible that I had on a dusty shelf. Randomly and without any thought (I was not in the habit of reading the Bible), I opened and read a Psalm (I don't remember which one exactly) that told me to have faith.

So, as soon as my EH left home, I sought help from my friends, and a co-worker invited me to go to her church. It was close to my home so I decided to go. The first day I went there, it was a service of praise and prayer and I heard praise that I never forgot "Restoration." There's no doubt that God was speaking to me so that I would not give up on my marriage and my family.

So, my restoration journey started, even before I found RMI. And it was neither easy nor quick.

I discovered RMI two months after that. A student of mine, who was facing separation, sent me the book How God Can and Will Restore Your Marriage as a pdf. I read the book in 2 days and cried buckets of tears each time I read it. I learned how guilty I had been for the collapse of my marriage and my family. I was very contentious, proud, independent ... My EH even told me that I was beautiful, intelligent, strong, independent, and did not need any man. But it was not due to my dependence on a Savior but due to the feminist attitude, most women have today. God began to remove the blindfold from my eyes. Soon after reading the RYM book, I quit therapy when I saw how what she told me was so opposite to what God said and what RMI opened my eyes to.

After reading the book, I searched the RMI website, signed up to get the daily encourager and started taking course 1. Within a month, my relationship with my EH started to improve. We didn't fight anymore because I stopped trying to get my own way and actually listened. The next improvement was when he came over right after the New Year and we were intimate, which was huge because he couldn't even stomach being in the same house with me. I began begging God to take all the anger out of my heart and as I did, my EH started approaching me, seeing I wasn't the same person he'd left. But there were several trials and I failed many times and it felt like I wasn't ever going to change or let go entirely. But my HH didn't give up on me. Lovingly He brought more hard trials into my life that almost made me give up but He knew it would break the hardness from my heart. And to soften the blow, at the same time He always sent me something like a praise report, a promise, or a message from someone that made me get up and keep moving along in my journey.

What principles, from God's Word (or through our resources), Jasmine, did the Lord teach you during this trial?

I think faith was the biggest principle in my RJ. Each day it grew inside me, and little by little, the fear of being alone (like my mother) was overcome. I also asked God many times to make me feel the Lord was truly my HH. I didn't want to suffer anymore. I learned how beneficial fasting was. And how my tithe would mean the Lord would protect me. And I started reading the Bible, all the way through, not just bits and pieces here and there. I have read the entire Bible once and am half way through the second time. I began by reading the Psalms and Proverbs you provide every day—and I fell in love with the Word of God! All the principles of life are there right where you tell us they are, all of our blessings and duties are there, it is so simple. I started talking about God to my daughters and teaching them to talk to Him as a Heavenly Father and to take all their fears to Him. I also learned to do this too. And, little by little, I was transformed without realizing it.

What were the most difficult times that God helped you through, Jasmine?

The last year before the restoration happened, without a doubt, the worst phase of my journey. My summer, as Erin calls it began when my EH had approached me about returning, but I was not yet ready. Then, the greatest trial came, I saw him with an OW (other woman). At first, I thought it was nothing serious, but then I found out that he had already introduced the OW to his family as a girlfriend and, on his birthday, she was at his party. My worst fear was imagined. When I discovered our daughters had met her and to protect me, hid meeting her from me. My reaction was not very good. I slid into a deep depression. Worse, I went back to seeing doctors for medication and a new psychologist. Awful. I lost a lot all due to my foolishness. But it was after all that my Lord restored me. I always knew that only He could heal me and, although I sought to be cured by men, I asked my HH (Heavenly Husband) to get rid of all that and He led me to begin fasting. Shortly thereafter, I don't know when, I started to feel better and better and was able to perform all my daily tasks again, and most importantly, my EH was no longer the focus of my attention. I had finally let go. This was clearly what it took.

"He said, 'You must obey [or listen to the voice of] the Lord your God and do what He says is right [is right in His eyes/sight]. If you obey all His commands [statutes; ordinances; requirements] and keep His rules, I will not bring on you any of the sicknesses [diseases] I brought on the Egyptians. I am the Lord who heals you [your Physician].'" Exodus 15:26 EXB

Jasmine, what was the "turning point" of your restoration?

It happened on my birthday. I planned to spend it alone with my daughters. We planned to have lunch at a restaurant, then go to the cinema and finally, I bought a cake to eat with them at home that evening. As it says, "The mind of man plans his way but the Lord directs his steps" Proverbs 16:9. During lunch my EH called and asked why we were having lunch at a nearby restaurant and I simply said I didn't want to make food that day (he didn't remember it was my birthday and I didn't want to tell him). However, I was not sad but thankful to be with my HH and my daughters. That's when my oldest daughter took her cell phone and called her father and asked if he knew what day it was. Then he remembered, called me again, apologized, wished me "Happy Birthday" and asked if he could be invited to have cake with us that evening. I agreed and when he came, he brought his parents, his aunt and our nephews. After that day, he started to come over more and more.

Tell us HOW it happened, Jasmine? Did your husband just walk in the front door? Jasmine, did you suspect or could you tell you were close to being restored?

A month after my birthday, it was summer vacation and our daughters were traveling with my EH's parents. While they were gone, he got quite sick and I went over to take care of him. I spent three days taking care of him and I realized that if he was still dating, surely his girlfriend would have taken care of him, but I didn't ask. After that, he started to invite me to come over to his parents' house, where he lived, and went back to talking about looking for an apartment so we could live together again. Today, we live in a brand new home. Not only is our home new, so is my husband. He goes shopping for us, fixes things, and helped paint our daughter's room. What's amazing is that it happened just like the other restored women say, when I didn't expect it to happen, when I really no longer wanted it because my HH was all I needed or wanted. It happened all of a sudden and am just so happy with just my HH.

Would you recommend any of our resources in particular that helped you, Jasmine?

Everything. The books How God Can and Will Restore Your Marriage, A Wise Woman, Questions and Answers, the daily encourager, and the courses. Indeed, this Ministry teaches us all the principles to go through our RJ. The fact that this is all free to us after being ruined by paying enormous amounts of money for therapy that never helped but only hurt me! It's such a testament to the power of God's Word and His ways being higher than our ways!

"My thoughts are nothing like your thoughts," says the Lord. "And my ways are far beyond anything you could imagine. For just as the heavens are higher than the earth, so my ways are higher than your ways and my thoughts higher than your thoughts." Isaiah 55:8–9

Would you be interested in helping encourage other women, Jasmine?

Yes!!

Either way, Jasmine, what kind of encouragement would you like to leave women with, in conclusion?

Have faith. Never give up on your marriages and your families. They are God's projects for your life. Follow the teachings of RMI, read the Bible, seek God always before everything and ask Him to become your Heavenly Husband. Teach your children to trust their Heavenly Father to be with them. Our HH is wonderful! With Him we have everything!

Chapter 19

Yennu

"He will yet fill your mouth with laughter,
And your lips with joyful shouting."
—Job 8:21

"I Hope to Pass My Victory Baton to You"

Yennu, how did your Restoration Journey actually begin?

PRAISE THE LORD He has turned my husband's heart back to us!

With this testimony, I want to begin by thanking our beloved Father and my HH (Heavenly Husband)! I also want to thank the creators of this website because it helped me so much and continues to help me due to the daily testimonies and devotions that keeps me encouraged. It's our spiritual food we need every day. May the Lord bless you! Now to share my journey...

When we got married I only focused on myself, almost entirely on my big wedding, without ever considering my husband's dreams or even about our future as a couple. This was horrible for my EH (earthly husband) because he could never count on me to help in the planning or construction of our new house and so many other needs we had as a couple. And due to this, he walked away from the ways of the Lord.

Fast forward to almost 12 years later, a year ago in March, when I was suddenly unemployed, and as soon as I got paid for 5 years of work, everything was gone once all of our previous debts and loans were paid. My EH was discouraged and tired of fighting an uphill battle alone, and that's when he told me that our marriage was over. But immediately, he told me to be patient because these feelings would pass. But I was foolish, quarrelsome, anxious and talked too much, complaining and impatient demanding that he commit to us.

What's worse, I told everything that was going on to his family, which made the situation much much worse. Six months later, in September, he left home. I was desperate and inconsolable despite the fact that during those 6 months he lived with us, but whined because he was no longer "present" as my husband.

Then it happened, in November, I found out on Facebook that he had become involved with his teenage ex-girlfriend. I was finally broken. God finally got my attention.

How did God change your situation, Yennu, as you sought Him wholeheartedly?

Even though I was already knowledgeable in His Word and it had increased since when we first met and got married—I desperately needed much more maturity, along with closeness and intimacy with our Lord, as my Heavenly Husband, HH. So I continued in the presence of the Lord and I searched with all my strength. I was praying night and day and made sure I woke up at 5 am in order to pray for hours before going to work. That allowed me to (during the workday) meditate on His Word all the time, while I was at work and during my commute.

One day I discovered testimonies of restored marriages on the internet and I found the most precious GIFT from RMI, the book How God Can and Will Restore Your Marriage. I read the whole book and reread it and each time I read it, I continued to become a woman I never knew could exist. Through this book, I started to pray using His Word for my husband, and even better, the Lord began to transform me into a woman I knew I needed to be. I simply asked Him (and I am still in the process of restoring my life and who He wants me to be). Making myself not the center of my world and putting love into practice, being patient with everyone, is such a joy—which also freed me from compulsive spending. I learned to free myself from my EH and cling only to our HH.

What principles, from God's Word (or through our resources), Yennu, did the Lord teach you during this trial?

The daily reading of the Word. Trusting in the Lord's promises. I learned to let go and wait on the Lord. The book How God Can and Will Restore Your Marriage and the testimonies of praise helped me a lot along this journey. Now I hope to pass my Victory baton to you who are reading my testimony.

What were the most difficult times that God helped you through, Yennu?

When he told me the marriage was over and he didn't love me anymore and when I found out he was involved with another woman. But the Lord in His infinite mercy supported me and didn't let me give up but each time to press more into intimacy with Him. Several times I thought about giving up. What surprised me that at one point I was even encouraged by the RMI to give up—but give it to Him. That's when I really felt free and He began to really change things!

Yennu, what was the "turning point" of your restoration?

As I prayed, fasted, and applied the principle of letting go fully, making my HH all I wanted, needed and Who I lived for, that's when the Lord began to turn my husband's heart to begin to look for me. In December he started to send me messages wanting to know how I was and if I would forgive him. Then in February he started coming home and stayed a while but always left. I found it strange and confusing, but then RMI reminded me it's a spiritual battle and to want HIM above all else to bring this Restoration Journey to the fork in the road and begin my Abundant Life Journey, praise God!

Tell us HOW it happened, Yennu? Did your husband just walk in the front door? Yennu, did you suspect or could you tell you were close to being restored?

The Lord had spoken in my heart that he would return on our anniversary, but I wasn't sure which anniversary. Yet by this time I wasn't sure I really wanted restoration because my HH and I were so in love. I was going to take a vacation from work and on our wedding anniversary, when he called and asked to spend the night at home. That night he said he would not be leaving again and asked if it was okay if he could go to get his belongings to stay at home. Glory to God, that was many months ago. Even though it's more difficult having him home as RMI tells us over and over, God says, "For I am confident of this very thing, that He who began a good work among you will complete it by the day of Christ Jesus." Philippians 1:6.

Would you recommend any of our resources in particular that helped you, Yennu?

Yes, take the courses, especially Finding Abundant Life. The book How God Can and Will Restore Your Marriage is where to start and A Wise Woman is the foundation to your changing. Reading the Word, reading the Daily Encourager and the Testimonies will pinpoint the areas of your lives. And to know how to get deeper into knowing the Lord, all recommended all of the Abundant Life courses.

Would you be interested in helping encourage other women, Yennu?

Yes, I'm available.

Either way, Yennu, what kind of encouragement would you like to leave women with, in conclusion?

Do not give up your Marriage. Let GOD fight for you while you focus on the Lord because He is our Rock.

Believe the Word, take them as the Lord's promises. Just take possession of them because they are yours.

"You will stand by and watch as the magnificence of this new house will eclipse the magnificence of My first house. And in this new house, I will give you peace." Haggai 2:9 Voice

"He will once again fill your mouth with laughter and your lips with shouts of joy." Job 8:21 NLT

You beloved who want your marriage restored, do not lose hope...persevere in the search for the Lord and call on Him, He will hear you. Remember if our God allowed this journey in your life it's because He Job 8:21 NLT wants to teach you to be the woman He created you to be and that you should become more intimate with Him and know Him as your Lover. All desert experiences aren't bad, enjoy the hot temperatures. Be eager to learn and understand what God's good "will" is for your life. The Lord has no pleasure in divorce! Malachi 2:16

Chapter 20

Fay

"The one who has found his life will lose it,
and the one who has lost his life on
My account will find it."
—Matthew 10:39

"We are in Our New Home Together!"

Fay, how did your Restoration Journey actually begin?

My EH (earthly husband) and I separated in December, almost a year ago after finding out about the OW (other woman). I made the decision to leave and move into an apartment with our two small children (at the time ages 2 yrs and 2 months). It was the toughest decision I ever had to make and looking back I should have stayed—even though I felt a ton of pain and anger. On New Year's Eve, I watched a prophetic prayer call and wrote in the chat for prayers concerning marriage and my husband. This woman responded and told me to check my messenger. She asked for my email and sent me a copy of the book How God Can and Will Restore your Marriage. She was upfront and let me know that this book was something serious and to be ready.

How did God change your situation, Fay, as you sought Him wholeheartedly?

At first, I wasn't seeing any change because my heart was still cold from the pain I felt after being married to someone for 4 years and together for 11 years. But once God started to reach me and reveal things about myself, I could slowly see the tide turning and my husband starting to soften. I began to take my eyes off of what happened and wanted to change and seek God and His relationship with me. I realized God was working on me and the intimate relationship I desperately needed with Him.

What principles, from God's Word (or through our resources), Fay, did the Lord teach you during this trial?

During this trial, God taught me a few things. First and foremost was to seek Him for everything and put no one else before Him. I never realized that I idolized my husband and put him before God. He also showed me the type of woman I was throughout our marriage (contentious, argumentative, nagging, and so on) and that I needed to change to be gentle, quiet, and still. (This is still my area of focus today but I'm quicker to notice when I'm starting to show these things).

What were the most difficult times that God helped you through, Fay?

Some of the most difficult times were when I wouldn't hear from my EH and my mind would begin to wonder. Also, the nights were hard and when I cried the most—but prayer truly helps and God will give you peace.

Fay, what was the "turning point" of your restoration?

I can't really pinpoint the exact turning point but I did begin to notice things my husband would say that he never would say about me. He began calling every morning and texting throughout the day. He even began talking about purchasing a home together as a family.

Tell us HOW it happened, Fay? Did your husband just walk in the front door?

He definitely did not just walk through the door but we began to seriously start talking about purchasing the home and nailed down a time to secure the loan. He looked for homes all by himself and chose a home that he thought would be perfect for us and our children. The entire process was tough because my EH would doubt his decisions and even mention the OW often but God prevailed and we are in our new home together! Although we are restored and back together, the battle is still being fought. God is still dealing with me but I will say I'm quicker to repent and also seek Him. This journey is very hard but I know God will win the battle and receive all of the glory for our marriage.

Fay, did you suspect or could you tell you were close to being restored?

I really couldn't tell because everything was so up and down. We would be having really good days and then really bad days. My EH was struggling with his decision and still does today. At times I grow weary but each time God always pulls me back in and closer to Him.

Would you recommend any of our resources in particular that helped you, Fay?

I recommend every resource!! The book How God Can and Will Restore your Marriage, and read it several times. The testimonies of other women were such an inspiration and glimmer of hope and the journals which helped me track my thoughts throughout the journey.

Would you be interested in helping encourage other women, Fay?

Absolutely!

Either way, Fay, what kind of encouragement would you like to leave women with, in conclusion?

This journey is very hard and it may seem like it will never get better but God is a faithful God and He will win the battle and receive all the Glory. Take this time to build an intimate relationship with God and become the woman He has called you to be. He cares so deeply for you and wants to give you the desires of your heart especially when it comes to your marriage. Your husband can be won without words!

Dear Brides,

There is nothing better than the unconditional love of God. He longs to give you the life you desire if you just trust in Him. Give Him your all (worries, concerns, praise, etc.) for He deserves the Glory. Once you give your life over to God and allow Him to be your Husband and you, His bride, He will change your heart and eventually the heart of your husband. Fall in love with Him, He is waiting for you. It's as simple as saying Yes!

"For we walk by faith, not by sight." (2 Cor. 5:7).

"Trust in the Lord with all thine heart; and lean not unto thine own understanding. In all thy ways acknowledge Him, and He shall direct thy paths." (Prov. 3:5–6 KJV).

"And we know that God causes all things to work together for good to those who love God, to those who are called according to His purpose." (Rom. 8:28).

He who has found his life will lose it, and he who has lost his life for My sake will find it. —Matthew 10:39

This scripture from Chapter 2 "Finding Your Life" says and means so much. Our life is not our own, but it belongs to God. We have to die to ourselves and give Him complete and total control. Once you do this, you will be able to experience the life and love He desires to give you.

In this chapter, I was able to see how important it is to live out your life for God. Once you delight yourself in the Lord and live according to His purpose and His Word, you will begin to experience the life He has in store. Take all of your concerns, worries and even your thanks to Him for He deserves all the glory and will carry you. Reading this has helped me to take everything I encounter to God (even my good stuff). No longer do I worry or depend on man because God will see me through and cover me. This has changed my heart, my way of thinking, and how I treat others.

The current struggles, just prior to my restoration, were thinking about my EH and what he may have been doing during our time of separation (i.e. is he with another woman, is he thinking about me and his children, etc). I have given my concerns to God and immediately feel a sense of peace in the entire situation. I pray to God to help me remove those thoughts and replace them with positive ones. He covers me and doesn't allow me to go to those dark places as I did in the past. It has helped me to focus on God alone and not reach out to my husband and respond in my old ways.

Going forward, especially now after my restoration, I will take all of my concerns to HIM. He is the answer to everything. Oftentimes when I seek Him especially in what I should do, He guides me. If He is quiet, then I know that I should wait to respond or react to certain situations. In the past, I did not live by the principles. I used to immediately try to handle issues on my own by consulting my HH (Heavenly Husband).

Dear Brides,

Delight yourselves in Lord! Not only for your marriage but for your entire life. He is your Healer, your Deliverer, your Refuge, your

Strength, your Guidance, your EVERYTHING. He will guide and provide for you in ways no one ever could.

This book and Finding the Abundant Life Course has been a true eye-opener for me as a wife. It brings you closer to God and changes you in ways that are unbelievable.

Chapter 21

Francisca

"For the wages of sin is death,
but the free gift of God is eternal
life in Christ Jesus our Lord."
—Romans 6:23

"Between Slaps and Kisses, Our First Child was Born"

Francisca, how did your Restoration Journey actually begin?

In the past I would answer without blinking that everything started on the honeymoon, today I know it was even before I got married. My sins condemned my marriage even before I got married. One sin begat the next sin, which gave birth to the next, and a string of sins established the destruction of my marriage. (An abyss calls another abyss, Psalm 42:7). I am the daughter of the world, I was raised with the values and bad habits of the world—generations of sin is how my life began and was fostered.

For you to understand better, my part in this tragic and so painful story, it all started with dishonor and disobedience to my parents in my teens, which left me blind, without discrimination, dead. "Honor your father and your mother; and: Whoever curses his father or mother will surely die." Matthew 15:4

Dishonor, coupled with wrong values, worldly thoughts, and goals were the cause of destruction. To feel loved, cherished, valued, I started dating very early, after I had a few boyfriends, and wrongly gave my heart, my strength, and mind to one of them, I did it with each that followed. After a while, one boy left me for another girl. At the time I suffered too much, I even wanted to die, in the midst of this emotional mismatch I tried to find another greater love, because there was a saying in my world at the time that stated that "you only forget a great love, with a greater one." Yes, there was a Greater Love who could help me get over it but I was years from discovering this secret.

In this wrong search for another great earthly love, I started dating my husband. We both already worked, after 2 years of dating we discovered that I was pregnant. We promptly scheduled the wedding. It was a difficult decision because inwardly I believed that I had not yet forgotten my first great love. If all this inner confusion was not enough, on my honeymoon, my (now) husband, who was a gentleman during courtship, cooled, ignored me, and treated me badly. We fought so much on our honeymoon, it was so bad that on the way back all I thought about was breaking up.

When I talked to my mother, she had her heart hardened, because for her a broken marriage was a dishonor, a shame for the family. At the age of 21 without support from my mother, I reluctantly moved in with my husband to try to make this marriage work. Unfortunately, the coexistence continued to be with many fights and disputes, because we both came from a sinful foundation, with habits of dishonor and disrespect, financial indiscipline, which resulted in having financial problems in the first month. Add this to our other problems, the main problem of mutual respect, we even physically attacked each other a few times. Verbal aggression was constant.

Between slaps and kisses, our first child was born. Two months later, I was already pregnant again. One son was born in January and the next in December of the same year. A widespread mess, a lot of financial and emotional mismatch. Things improved a little bit financially, and we had our third child two years later. More and more fights, more disagreements, everything always revolving around finances, immaturity, and lack of respect.

Until we gave up on our own business, I quickly got a job, we went to live at my parents' house because of expenses, but my husband didn't get any job. He didn't even really make a move to look for one, on the contrary, he had a thousand excuses, which I saw as a weak man I was tied down to.

Four years went by in this huge mess, every year I was getting more tired of the whole situation. I wanted to leave my parents house, as it was supposed to be temporary, just a few months while we were reorganizing our lives. But he was enjoying the comfort, the lack of responsibility, the support we had there. I believe that he did not have a family like that and what for my husband was a treat, for me, it was becoming a calamity. A little bit of me died every day. I wanted my own house, my own family, my privacy, and peace—because my parents fight too much, they had a marriage full of fights. They fought so much that they didn't even realize how much they fought and in front of all of us.

Over the four years we lived in my parents' house, the situation became impossible for me. I was still very young, with 3 small children, and in my head, I was condemned to a marriage where my parents and I were the providers, while my husband enjoyed staying at home and being taken care of. He didn't even take care of his own children. After asking, begging my husband, my mother to talk to my husband, appealing to any and all human decency, to leave my parents' house and support his family. Nothing we did was successful.

I was hurt, worn out, exhausted, and on the edge.

How did God change your situation, Francisca, as you sought Him wholeheartedly?

"I want you to show mercy, not offer sacrifices. For I have come to call not those who think they are righteous, but those who know they are sinners." Matthew 9:13 "God's kindness leads him to repentance." Romans 2:4

In the midst of this agony of life, I was consumed within, destroyed. I cried in secret, I didn't talk to anyone anymore, and I couldn't see a way out. I was trapped. Trapped in a prison of pain, lies, deception, guilt, condemnation, hatred, resentment, and endless hurts. But God...

My dear Heavenly Husband, Wonderful, My Eternal Prince of Peace, finally provided a way for my EH to have his own business, and during the interviews that he went on throughout the following year, I said "if God works, if my EH gets a job without having any degree, I will go to church, I will know that God exists, God sees me. If He shows me that I exist because only He can solve this huge mess, I go to church and I will never leave Him again." He started his own business at the end of the year our 3rd child was born, and in the same month I grabbed him and his 3 children, and we all went to church.

At the first church service, I told God that He needed to prove to me that He was real once and for all or if it was an illusion, unrealistic. In my mind, I said that from now on I would do everything in my power, that I would obey Him unconditionally, that I would obey all 10 commandments and that I would tithe, that I would never make a decision again without His approval. That was my part, His was to prove that He was real. See I was not being boastful, and He knows that, understand my context, I had been raised in the Catholic Church, going to countless masses, saying rosaries, making many promises to saints, the Christ I knew was nailed to the wall and did not interact with people. I was desperate for a saviour, a saviour just for me! I was filthy, weighed down with sin, overwhelmed by guilt and condemnation. I now hated myself more than I hated my husband because I was the person who committed adultery - an adulterous woman in our society is considered a prostitute. Neither society nor my family would have room and mercy for me, I would be emotionally stoned to death. I needed to know if God was real because He would have a solution, and I was giving Him everything I knew existed, including that part of the tithe. I had never heard tithe in the Catholic church, but I had a lot of financial problems, so it was all or nothing, I was throwing myself into death (if He didn't exist and all that was just man's invention).

Five months later God led me to be born again, He washed my soul, washed my guilt, washed away all the accusations, fears, pain, anger. He tore the sky and poured out love abundantly in my life. He was speaking to my heart and teaching me more about God, His Grace, His Favor, His Justice, His desire to save me, this infamous sinner. I cried every day, all day, when I was supplied with love, supplied with self-forgiveness, supplied with grace. He gave me the main command that changed my whole life.

God explained that love is a command we choose to obey or ignore. We must decide to obey and love a person, even if he is not worth loving and we don't feel anything for that person. Love does not depend on feeling, that love is a verb, a continuous attitude. I will love as He loves me. The person decides to love, to obey the command, and in obedience, the feeling will appear. He then explained to me what constitutes true love, how this verb multiplies in actions, actions, and not feelings, "Love is patient and kind. It is not envious, nor proud; it is not arrogant, nor rude. Love does not demand that you do what he wants."

"Love is patient and kind. It is not envious, nor proud; it is not arrogant, nor rude. Love does not demand that you do what it wants. It is not irritable and hardly suspicious of the harm that others can do to you. Never is He satisfied with injustice, but he rejoices in the truth. Love never gives up, never loses faith, always has hope, and perseveres in all circumstances." 1 Corinthians 13:4-6

I was shocked, because my whole life I believed in love as an overwhelming feeling, in the love that I watched on soap operas, in the movies, love based on body chemistry. However, my Savior, and now He was the Lord, explains in His Word that love is a verb, an action, a daily practice that begins in the heart, the person's decision to obey God. I was shocked that I had decided to obey God to death, never to do anything without God's permission, authorization, and blessing. And what I prayed the most in these last 5 months was when I could officially separate, when that lie, my marriage would end, that God would show me the right time for separation. And He was actually preparing me to receive the message that He hates divorce and that this insane marriage, conceived entirely in sin and error, was a marriage that He wanted me to remain in and flourish in.

The prison of lies that held me captive was in an instant destroyed, I was freed from lies, deception, darkness.

What principles, from God's Word (or through our resources), Francisca, did the Lord teach you during this trial?

God needed to teach me everything because I knew nothing. Seeking God first, reading and obeying His word saved my life. The principles that are in your wonderful book, How God Can and Will Restore Your Marriage, the loving book (Bible) was what finally taught me to live a decent, honest, upright life and how to relate to myself, the people around me, and especially my husband. The first lesson after I returned home with my mindset on God's plan, was to shut up, not to answer back when my husband spoke to me anymore. Pray, and read the Bible daily to learn about this new plan, this new life I was living—this new opportunity that had been revealed to me, but that I didn't understand or knew almost nothing about.

Then RMI entered my life where I learned to let go, and to agree with the enemy, to look to the Lord as a Heavenly Husband. This was the second most amazing gift of my life after receiving my salvation!!

What were the most difficult times that God helped you through, Francisca?

There were many, so many. So I will briefly describe a few. The first was we had our business that went bankrupt, so all of our financial support was taken away and everything was slowly being taken from us. The more I prayed and fasted, the worse the situation got. We are left with huge debts in the courts, the banks, and to our family. This tribulation lasted 10 years, we were very crushed, ashamed, but in the end, I learned to depend on God financially and to wait for Him to complete His plan.

One point that culminated in breaking me, and that put me back to bed, in depression, in sadness, was when I realized that many years had passed since my conversion and the rescue of my marriage, however, my husband had left the church, being soon followed by our children who were teenagers at the time. This second depression was lighter than the first, I started to fight it with prayer, no medication, or counseling. I tried everything until HE guided me to RMI.

I was hungry for a clear direction, where the Bible was the sole guide (or soul guide :) I quickly took all the courses online, read the book A Wise Woman, and started helping other women. That was the biggest breakthrough. My mind started a new process of renewal, of purification, I began noticing all wrong concepts I accepted as truth from other Christians and churches, but due to your materials and urging us to get in His Word and ask Him, I began to form new mental strengths. God became my source for wisdom and a new process of brokenness, healing, and liberation in my life was established, as well as, in my emotions and in my family.

I had already talked about God so much with all the members of the home, that I managed to burn all the opportunities because the previous speech was not compatible with my behavior. I was a Pharisee and a contentious woman too. Once I began the process of meekness, humility, patience, being very quiet, waiting for what God wanted me to do or say, when He wants me to do it, and how He wants to do it, then I began to be effective with the people I knew who came to me and asked me!

It was very difficult to admit that I was still a fool in many areas of my life, that after so many years of serving God, confessing everything is always helpful because it is a new beginning. RMI has helped in this process of reconnecting me with my first Love, my HH, and realizing our lives are always on the road to restoration. I had been stuck in a ditch for a long time and couldn't even understand what I was doing wrong. Encouraging me to journal, to confess, to pour my heart out to Him whenever I learned something new kept me moving along quickly and peacefully.

It was very difficult to deal with my EH's indifference at various stages of our marriage, however, the principle of receiving everything you need from your HH, His affection, His love, sustains me, and keeps me encouraged, inspired, protected from my EH when he's not who I know he would like to be. Everything I need comes from Him. Focus on Him, look to Him, expect what only He can give you, and not EH. Also, learn to Let Go. Leave it with Him.

Francisca, what was the "turning point" of your restoration?

The initial turning point was to repent and receive the son of God as Lord, Savior, Redeemer, and Director of my life, to give Him the first place in Everything. Receiving the Good News, the truth, forgiveness, and His Word as the center of my life.

The current turning point remains exactly the same, repenting and restoring the Lord as my First Love, as my HH, as the center of my entire existence. "But I have this against you that you left your first love." Revelation 2:4. Somehow I had lost myself, even behind the values of the church and the promises of God, I believe that I lost myself in my own understanding, with the deadlines we give and with fantasies we create. Letting go of the church puts Him in first place.

My life took a turn when I returned to my first Love, and finally discovered that He was not only my Redeemer, Lord, Father, King, but mainly He was my Perfect Husband, the Heavenly Husband who had a covenant with me—a perfect, unbreakable covenant.

Tell us HOW it happened, Francisca? Did your husband just walk in the front door? Francisca, did you suspect or could you tell you were close to being restored?

Yes, my husband just showed up, or maybe it was I who showed up. I didn't see anything was about to happen. I was blind, and God did everything Himself. Without my help, without interference. I got in the way. It is just as your book says it's how GOD will restore, we can't.

Would you recommend any of our resources in particular that helped you, Francisca?

I highly recommend all of your online courses, they are fundamental in renewing and cleansing the mind and soul. mind renewal. I took each course several times, and I believe I will still do them again and again.

I recommend the book A Wise Woman, what a gem. Reading the daily Encourager, the daily devotionals, and reading the Bible every day (greatest book on LOVE in the universe)!

Would you be interested in helping encourage other women, Francisca?

Yes, totally interested.

Either way, Francisca, what kind of encouragement would you like to leave women with, in conclusion?

Beloved and beautiful women, the encouragement I leave you with is that no one has loved you or will never love you like your Heavenly Husband longs to love you. Until you believe and receive this truth as the first of your life, and it becomes the cornerstone of your life, you will continue to be submerged in pain and torment.

All the love that you wanted to receive, all the affection, all the acceptance, all the pain, all the abandonment, the contempt that you feel, all the emptiness that is tearing at your heart. Everything that you think was your EH who caused it, everything is for your HH (Heavenly Husband) to take care of— your EH (earthly husband) will never be able to take or fix anything.

Our heart belongs to the KING, our life is His, our everything must remain with our Heavenly Husband.

I deeply thank Him for first showing me that I needed Him—for so many years of my life. And that He chose the fools of this world to confuse the wise. He took me as His, He poured out His wisdom and love on me. And then He chose to test me, poured rain on me, caused rivers to overflow, to blow the winds from all sides, but He has kept me grounded in Him who is my Rock and my salvation.

"So whoever hears these words of mine and practices them is like a prudent man who built his house on the rock. The rain fell, the rivers overflowed, the winds blew and hit that house, and it did not fall, because it had its foundations on the rock" Matthew 7:24, 25

Chapter 22

Sophia

"Do not be amazed that I said to you,
'You must be born again.'"
—John 3:7

"Restoration was Impossible because I was Dirty Before God"

Sophia, how did your Restoration Journey actually begin?

Well, I don't exactly know how it started. But I remember very well that a few months ago I was in a situation that was "very difficult and impossible" in the eyes of the world. I had already given up everything since we weren't together anymore, so when we parted, even though I was still in love I thought "there is no reason why I should be eaten up with remorse because of this, I am young and I will find another husband who is even better." So I remained steadfast for a few months with these ideas, but inside it just didn't feel quite right. Looking back, God had already prepared everything and it began to unfold.

A new internship opportunity arose that I heard was being offered in another department. I was currently working inside the factory and did not have time to go online because at home I am without internet. But when I changed departments, I started to have more time to go on the internet during my breaks. I often researched things, including the singles pages looking for someone new. Then one day I found the book How God can and Will restore your marriage. I downloaded the book and sent it to my phone and every day I read it. But I didn't know there was an official webpage, so in another research, I found your site.

When I told my story in the questionnaire, a few days later the team replied saying "nothing is impossible" and I sat there amazed! Could this be true? I thought why not try, so I started doing the first course. I could sense that God was always there, with me, guiding me just like you said. And I took the principles from the book to heart and applied each to my life.

How did God change your situation, Sophia, as you sought Him wholeheartedly?

God shook up many things in me. First, He made me clean! I always felt dirty and one day that was particularly horrible for me, I found the page Crisis Corner and then felt Him lead me to go back to reread about my Divine Appointment again on Hope At Last. There I read something I'd skipped over the first time, "Are you looking for a 'peace' that surpasses ALL understanding?" and I said, "Yes!" I kept reading and when I read the verse, "Do not marvel that I said to you, 'You must be born again.' Jesus just before that answered and said to him, 'Truly, truly, I say to you, unless one is born again, he cannot see the kingdom of God'" — John 3:7 It finally made sense to me. I cannot explain how I felt!!

The way I always thought about things, and the limitation that I had about our God, I only knew Him superficially. God transformed me in an instant! I felt clean, alive, free. I wrote to your ministry and they suggested finding Him as my First Love. So I started your Abundant Life courses. I also started to read the Bible more and pray more, to seek Him as first place in my life. He also led me to begin fasting, which helped me gain that gentle and quiet spirit that I never understood before. It was not easy, but I started to put my HH in the forefront of my mind and I was willing to wait for the rest of His plan to unfold.

What principles, from God's Word (or through our resources), Sophia, did the Lord teach you during this trial?

One of the principles is obedience to God and letting go. God taught me that I can only change and transform my life if I obey Him, and to let go of any and every situation that worries me. GOD showed me that I don't need to create any circumstances for Him to act. I simply need to ask Him to do it and He does. Sometimes I have to wait, but He is always faithful. I learned to be meek, quiet, and to forgive and love my neighbor, which meant to me everyone in my life, including strangers.

What were the most difficult times that God helped you through, Sophia?

The most difficult times were at the beginning of the journey when I had to understand God's plans for my life, letting my husband go, giving him no sign of my desire for him, and having a ready answer to the questions that everyone asked, "Are you dating anyone new?" Because as He became first, I looked so happy and everyone thought I was with someone new. I began telling everyone, "Well, yes, I have met someone new" and would leave it at that. Only God knows what I went through to get to that place. Sometimes while I rested in the arms of the Most High my EH would call just to say hello. Sometimes he'd come over, but it was amazing that it always happened when I was with my HH (Heavenly Husband) and feeling content. Sometimes he stayed home for days without returning to the OW (other woman), and then just disappeared without a word. I didn't know what was going on, so I learned not to be too anxious and instead enjoy the time he was gone to spend time with my Beloved and relish in my new life with Him.

Sophia, what was the "turning point" of your restoration?

The turning point was when I just looked at my Heavenly Husband, prayed more and fasted and sang love songs just to calm my heart and come to a place in my journey where everything was a paradise! When I stopped worrying and was happy about having to wait, and when I was 100% sure I obeyed God. When I didn't want the restoration anymore, I just prayed that the will of God would be done. When I learned to be gentle and quiet, not only when I talked to my EH but with everyone around me. When I learned to respect others, to forgive and love the people around me, and to value what others did for me. GOD began to teach me to be someone different, more humble, less resentful.

Tell us HOW it happened, Sophia? Did your husband just walk in the front door? Sophia, did you suspect or could you tell you were close to being restored?

I never imagined that my restoration would be so fast. It was only 8 months that I searched fervently and everything changed in my life. It started by my EH (earthly husband) sending me msg very often, and then calling me to say that everything was not ok. He stated several times how much better it had been with me, which was exactly the verse I prayed.

"He will pursue his lovers, but he will not overtake them; and he will seek them, but will not find them. Then he will say, 'I will go back to my first love (and I'd put my name in) for it was better for me then than now!'" Hosea 2:7

What's amazing is that because He changed me and I am now quiet and meek, I did not say anything. Instead, I just smiled and thanked God for how faithful He is. So he started to ask me out, to visit his friends with him, then a short time later, when we were talking together, he told me about a house he'd bought. While I waited for God to finish what He began, I gave myself completely to God, I threw myself at the heart of my HH and prayed that after 21 days of fasting that I would hear the good news.

God acted on my behalf and we moved into our new home before my fast ended. God changed my life, giving back hope. I, who entered here at RMI and thought restoration was impossible because I was dirty before God, and I failed a lot, did the impossible for me. God is good and He searches the hearts of those who seek Him. Thank You, my Love!

Would you recommend any of our resources in particular that helped you, Sophia?

The first book I recommend to everyone is how God can and will restore your marriage, then the courses, and a wise woman. Applying each principle in each of your books and courses are what changed me. What helped me the most was to always obey, not to seek blessings for ourselves, but first to seek a relationship with God and finding our HH as our first love from your Abundant Life courses. This is the greatest blessing... far above being restored. Having that relationship with your Beloved.

Would you be interested in helping encourage other women, Sophia?

I am interested, yes, always.

Either way, Sophia, what kind of encouragement would you like to leave women with, in conclusion?

I believe that in my testimony I did not tell even half of what happened to me. How can I ever explain the care that God administered to me? How He always answered me and the many battles He fought for me? First of all, read the book How God can and will restore your marriage, do not deviate from the Word and read it often to be cleansed, "so that He might sanctify her, having cleansed her by the washing of water with the Word" Ephesians 5:26.

Pray without ceasing, let go of your relationship, do not create any circumstances for God to act. Because the God we serve He has the power, so never doubt and no matter how long He takes to answer, remember He is always in control. I could see it all when I was "in the desert" and as crazy as it sounds, I still "miss it" because in the desert God teaches us, molds us, and brings us closer to Him and you can feel Him so close to you.

Start to be more dependent on Him, appreciate small details. Pray with all humility, exposing all the problems and difficulties in detail to Him and speak to no one else. Do not be ashamed to speak to God each time you have failed and where you have failed, always look to Him. And to finish, I'll leave these verses: "The plans of the heart belong to man, but the answer of the tongue is from the Lord." Proverbs 16:1

"...and if My people who are called by My name humble themselves and pray, and seek My face and turn from their wicked ways, then I will hear from heaven, will forgive their sin, and will heal their land." 2 Chronicles 7:14

Chapter 23

Manon

"Hardly had I left them When I found him
whom my soul loves; I held on to him
and would not let him go..."
—Song of Solomon 3:4

"I Told Him, No, I Wasn't Able to Let Go of My Lover"

Manon, how did your Restoration Journey actually begin?

It all started when I discovered my EH's (earthly husband) infidelity just after being married for almost 4 years. And rather than just ending things, I even tried to continue with our marriage. Until, one day, soon after we moved into our new home believing we were both very happy when he simply told me that he didn't love me anymore, that he didn't feel anything for me at all and he wanted a separation. The entire time he cried a lot, said that he did not know how this happened or why, and that he had already thought about disappearing just to be free of me. He told me because of what he was doing (but didn't say exactly what), that he couldn't do it anymore. Immediately I panicked, I didn't believe it would get to this point.

How did God change your situation, Manon, as you sought Him wholeheartedly?

At first I was desperate, I tried to stay at my job but I couldn't. I spent the whole day crying and praying I'd wander aimlessly on the streets of the city looking for a church so I could go to mass. I spent all my money on buses, on lighting candles at church, on Christian books that said something, anything about marriage and other things that I'd hope "could" help me. I didn't even feel what I was saying anymore while praying, my prayers were already automatic like a zombie. I lost 35 lbs, 15kg, in just 2 months. This was actually a good thing because I was overweight and it was something that bothered me and also upset my EH.

The entire time I trusted God. I have always trusted God a lot, even though I didn't know Him personally as I do today. But I knew that He was the One who could save my marriage. I accepted living in the desert and stayed with my Lord. I never looked for other doctrines, nor did I speak much with other people about my situation. Well, that's not entirely true I guess.

Early on, I went looking for a psychologist, but nothing she said touched my heart or gave me any peace at all. Glory to God for that, I ended up walking out while she was saying something because I trusted only the Lord, and nothing she said rang true. Then it all changed, in a single moment during my prayer at 3 am, the Lord led me to find RMI. The next day I downloaded the book and read it in just 2 days. From the beginning, I followed "all" principles, every single one. It was not difficult for me to follow, as I was already leading a more hidden life in God, focusing on Christian principles. But it was very important to discover all my mistakes that immediately began to help me make sense of how things had gotten so bad.

It was sad because I always thought I was the best wife, the best woman, and to discover that I was a Pharisee, contentious, an authoritarian, rebellious, a know-it-all, jealous, idolatrous (my marriage, my husband, money spent on a food obsession these were just a few of my idols) and countless other things I discovered each time I reread the book. It was painful discovering all these mistakes, and as for knowing that my marriage had been destroyed by my own hands, to discover that I was a foolish woman was both devastating and enlightening at the same time. It made me realize I wasn't a victim and my life could change and improve.

God is wonderful and is deserving of all honor, glory, praise, and worship. As I read the book, the testimonies, the Bible, and took the courses, God was forging, reshaping my character and I felt happy and at peace maybe for the first time in my life. The more I read, the more I wanted to become a woman after God's own heart. I wanted to be transformed to be a virtuous woman and have a marriage that would honor Him rather than pleasing me. I no longer wanted anything like the marriage I'd had, I wanted a new marriage founded on the Rock. God gave me the grace to be very patient, as waiting for God's appointed time it was surprisingly easy for me. Not that I didn't suffer, I suffered a lot, but I suffered drenched in His love, wanting more from God. More than everything, I longed for Him to transform my life and the life of my EH. To do for us what He'd done for me. I saw all of the Lord's promises being fulfilled in our lives and that delighted me every day. The God we serve is a wonderful God!!!

What principles, from God's Word (or through our resources), Manon, did the Lord teach you during this trial?

Presenting everything to Him, letting go, winning without words, and being humble were the principles that touched me the most. In the beginning, I was constantly tormenting my EH with messages, I watched his every move but when I read about the principle of letting go, I immediately stopped everything. It was harder to let it go in my heart, but with God's grace and mercy, I did it. The turning point was Finding the Abundant Life. Having your own Lover changes everything. Even before I was restored, I already missed the moments with the Lord and already asked Him not to let me get away from Him, and if necessary, allow everything again so that I could turn to Him alone. Glory to God! As I trusted the Lord more and more every day, just gave Him everything and literally rested on Him. Everything I experienced was wonderful ...

What were the most difficult times that God helped you through, Manon?

The most difficult times were when I was contacted by the OW (other woman). I'm so grateful that the Lord gave me a love for her after reading the OW was not the enemy The Other "Victim" During my journaling, I began asking Him to help me forgive her, (this is another wonderful testimony that I need to share). It was she who gave me news of my EH's involvement with her, the second was her sharing photos of them, but it only happened twice because I let go of social media Fasting Facebook so there was no way of her finding me. The other difficult times were when my EH started coming home and we had intimacy and he'd just up and leave right after. I felt used, despite the affection he had for me during our time together. I even asked God not to allow him to come over anymore, but God needed that to happen. So instead, I doubled up on my Abundant Life courses and that healed my heart! All Glory goes to Him! I was happy when he got up and left because I could be with my Lover who filled my heart.

Manon, what was the "turning point" of your restoration?

My EH started coming home a few times due to the difficulties he was going through (financially, and he was forced to let go of his apartment and live at his parents' house). Because he was depressed (even though it was a hit to his freedom and at the same time he felt good there) but he said, he felt the calmest and at peace at home with me. He always came and went without me saying anything. I came to the point when I relished when he left so I could be alone with my Beloved HH. I was very worried that he was so clearly depressed and doing lots of nonsense, but as I let go, I just held on even more to my HH and gave myself wholly to Him.

Tell us HOW it happened, Manon? Did your husband just walk in the front door? Manon, did you suspect or could you tell you were close to being restored?

No, I didn't imagine it was so close. It happened quite unexpectedly. I was staying in the city to participate in a woman's retreat. I'd set up the retreat for a group of women who were studying A Wise Woman and he called me asking what I was doing. I said I was with some friends staying in the city, and he said he wanted to meet me for dinner. I didn't want to just abandon my retreat, as I was the one who coordinated it, but after speaking to my Beloved HH, I sensed I needed to share it as a praise report with my group who said, GO. We met for dinner and it seemed he wanted to ask me something or tell me something. Later I found out he thought my "friends" was another man. He said he could tell I was "in love" so he didn't want to humiliate himself by asking to come home.

The day he came back home and moved his things in was actually the day of our wedding anniversary but I just didn't remember it was until a week later! I was amazed at God's appointed time. On his second day home, at breakfast, is when he asked what I thought about trying again. Could I forgive him? Could I become un-entangled with the man he said I knew I was involved with! I had to laugh, it was wonderful!!! My HH gave me the opportunity to share who I was "involved" with. I told him, No, I wasn't able to let go of my Lover when his face fell and I thought he would cry! Then I said I'd fallen head over heels in love with the Lord, and my transformation happened because of Him.

"When I found him whom my soul loves; I held on to him and would not let him go." Song of Solomon 3:4

So I told him that to continue to be transformed I needed ample time to be with Him. He agreed. One day later, while crying, he told me that he loved me and that the love he felt was much greater than what he felt at any time in our lives! My God, the Lord did wonders for me, it was much more than I thought he'd ever say.

We've been back together for 8 months now. Our marriage was restored after 2 ½ years of living apart and each day was so worth every single thing I went through! Thank You, Lord, you are my everything!!!

Would you recommend any of our resources in particular that helped you, Manon?

Certainly, everything you offer beginning with the book How God Can and Will Restore Your Marriage which is essential. The Word of God is indispensable and all your courses, your daily encourager and the book A Wise Woman were certainly gifts from God, given to me through Erin and RMI. Thank you for changing my life forever ...

I thank God for the life of Erin and all of the people at RMI ministry. I ask God to pour out unmeasured blessings on each of you and your families and on all who come to find hope from this ministry.

Would you be interested in helping encourage other women, Manon?

Yes for sure! As I have already mentioned, I have a group of Wise Women who study the book and share praise. We meet weekly and try to get away for a retreat every few months. I asked God early on to use me to bring hope to other women, to heal families and purchased 2 Wise Woman paperback books and just waited. I asked one woman and then she asked a friend and the group was formed and just continued to grow from there.

Either way, Manon, what kind of encouragement would you like to leave women with, in conclusion?

Beloved, trust totally in God and never take your eyes off Him, however difficult it may be. He is the God of the impossible, the God who keeps all His promises as He kept each of mine. Let Him change your life. Serve Him with love, let Him carry the cross for your marriage, and let

Him carry you. Never, never give up believing for restoration, do not give your husband's soul to the enemy, be sure you let God battle for him, for your marriage, for your children, for you. Live in obedience and cry out to God for transformation, for without it, everything will be as before.

Chapter 24

Annabella

"The steadfast of mind You will
keep in perfect peace,
Because he trusts in You."
—Isaiah 26:3

"2020 Covid, Hospitalized 2 Weeks, Intensive Care!"

Ministry Note: Prior to submitting her restored marriage testimony, Annabella submitted a praise report.

Dear Brides,

I would like to share a recent testimony. I cut my hand trying to charge my cell phone next to a chest of drawers with a detached back. Two days after my husband offered me to go with him to buy the Christmas presents for our children. Of course, it was a pleasure. We spent a beautiful afternoon together. In the evening my husband left and I went to pick up the children from school and the nursery. When I came back home I felt very feverish, I was shaking, I had a fever. I hesitated to call my husband. I prayed and said, "Lord, if I have to call him, give me a sign". The Lord made me think that I should take my temperature and once I took it I found out that I surely did have a fever.

So I decide to call my husband and ask him to come over and relieve me with the children. Then I lay on the couch with my husband by my side who was taking care of me. Once night fell, I woke up crying because of the pain in my right arm. I was crying and I told my husband I had to go to the hospital urgently. My husband then decided to call my sister to come and watch our children.

Because of the health crisis, my husband could not stay with me but the emergency doctors took my parameters and concluded that I had a covid infection. I was able to go home after having some drugs and a covid test (which the results were available the day after). I was sick and I knew in my heart that it was not covid. The next day, I was still, not feeling well and I vomited. The hospital called me back to tell me that I don't have the covid and asked me to come back urgently for more tests. Before leaving my house for the hospital I told my children: "Mommy is coming back, I'm going to the doctor pretty fast". Once there, my health deteriorated and I was taken to intensive care. I didn't really understand what was happening to me but I was serene.

At no time did I think I could never go home. There were several unexpected complications during my convalescence but I knew that my Heavenly Husband was faithful to His Word and I remembered only two verses:

"fear thou not, for I am with thee; be not dismayed, for I am thy God. I will strengthen thee; yea, I will help thee; yea, I will uphold thee with the right hand of My righteousness." (Isaiah 41:10 KJ21)

"And they shall fight against thee; but they shall not prevail against thee, for I am with thee," saith the Lord, "to deliver thee." (Jeremiah 1:19 KJ21)

I know that I am the apple of His eye and that He protects me. And that even if we have battles or trials, we are more than winners. Thus, despite this trial, I did not fear for my life, I knew that God, my God, was with me. So I wrote the verse of Isaiah on the white board in my room so that all the nurses could read it and know the goodness and power of my Heavenly Husband. And you know what? The doctors were amazed how quickly I recovered from my illness knowing all the complications that had developed. I didn't have Christmas with my family because I was in the hospital, which made me sad, but my Heavenly Husband had the perfect plan for me. After this trial, I can finally say that my marriage has been restored. (I will tell you more in my testimony).

What I have learned and had to relearn through this trial is not to look at my circumstances, however painful they may be, but to have faith in the word and keep my eyes on my Heavenly Husband. His plan is always perfect.

Annabella, how did your Restoration Journey actually begin?

First of all, I will explain my situation and how I got here. I met my husband when I was 21 years old. It was my first serious relationship. It was unexpected because the year I met him was the year before I went to live in the United States for a year. So it wasn't the right time for me to meet someone. At first, neither of us took the relationship seriously but soon we became closer and closer. I still went to the United States for a year and we broke up. When I came back to Belgium, we had reconnected and because the feelings were still there, we decided to get back together but that this time our relationship would be serious. We got engaged and moved in together 4 years later. My husband wanted to get married but I was not enthusiastic about the idea. Soon, a lot of arguments between us started. My husband's cousin asked us to come to a couple's meeting in her church.

We went and we liked it very much and slowly we became members of that church. After talking with the pastor we realized that we could no longer live like that, in sin, and that we should get married, but I got pregnant. So the wedding was postponed. We were a family now, with an adorable little boy, but the problems between us were still present. That said, we still wanted to get married like it was planned and we did it when my son was 2 and a half years old. And I immediately became pregnant with my daughter the day of my civil wedding. But again, the issues between my husband and me were still present. We didn't get along well enough, and slowly but surely we didn't speak to each other. Each of us was doing his own thing. Feeling ignored by my husband, I acted like him by ignoring him in return. I'll let you imagine the damage. But I had the desire to make things right, so I suggested to my husband to go see a marriage counsellor. It didn't take 4 sessions for my husband to decide to leave the house permanently and take off his wedding ring. I was so angry at him because I wanted to make things right this time and as soon as it was too difficult he dared to leave me. At least that's what I thought.

After a week of real anger and frustration, I was broken like never before. I was alone with two children, I had no money and I had lost my job because of the covid and I was sad. I looked for help on the internet and I don't know how I ended up on the website hopeatlast.com. I started reading all the courses and I realized I had to let go. Which I did immediately. I'm that kind of woman who makes drastic decisions quickly when it's really necessary. I apologized to my husband when he came to see the children. He came twice a week at first and he was sleeping at home in our bed and then one day he asked me not to be present when he came to see the children, which I did.

So as soon as he came to my house I would leave, and I would come back when he was about to leave. I made sure that dinner and the children were ready for him when he was there. Then step by step he was less cold with me and one day he told me that I didn't have to leave when he came to see the children at home. One day, he took a day off to pick up my son on a weekday and drop him off at my home just to see me. My son and my husband ate their lunch together and that day my husband didn't stop talking to me, he was seeking to interact with me. He was happy, he laughed a lot even if I wasn't making any jokes. That day, I understood that his heart had turned. And that same evening, for the first time, he sent me a text message to say that he missed me.

How did God change your situation, Annabella, as you sought Him wholeheartedly?

God did not directly change my situation, God broke me and made me rely only on Him and no other. It was a time where my faith was tested and I can't even tell you how, but I was happy and at peace. God showed me His mercy, He showed me that I didn't need anyone but Him and most importantly that with Him I already had everything. The funny thing is that I was able to be a witness for other people. When I was asked how I managed to be smiling despite everything, I answered: It's not me, it's God. When He works on our hearts, He does it so deeply that even we find it hard to believe how we are transformed.

What principles, from God's Word (or through our resources), Annabella, did the Lord teach you during this trial?

The first principle I learned was the discovery of my Heavenly Husband. I didn't know Him, I didn't know He was real and I didn't realize He was there for me. I enjoyed getting to know Him, talking to Him, and confiding in Him my feelings and doubts. It was magical and made me feel so good. He was there for me but that He will always be there for me. He became the love of my life.

The second principle is the principle of letting go. I think if the principle would have been "Run after my husband" I would not have been receptive. By nature, I don't like to chase after people and moreover, regarding my marriage, I was getting tired in this fight. Soon, I realized that I was getting tired because it was not mine to fight. I just had to lay down my burdens and do what the Lord tells me to do.

The third one is the principle of tithing in our storehouse. I had no idea how important it was to tithe in the right place.

What were the most difficult times that God helped you through, Annabella?

When my husband left I had just lost my job. I had no money, I couldn't pay my rent or go to the grocery store, I had bed bugs that had invaded my place and I had come down with shingles (a kind of chicken pox), to end the year 2020 hospitalized 2 weeks including a few days in intensive care for meningitis. 6 months was intense emotionally, spiritually and physically. All these moments were difficult and without God, I don't think I would have been able to survive.

Annabella, what was the "turning point" of your restoration?

The turning point was my hospitalization at the end of the year. For the first time since we became parents, my husband was alone for 2 weeks with our two children. I was not there, so he had to take care of everything. In addition, as my condition was critical at the beginning, he also had to protect our children by telling them that I was fine and that I was coming home even though neither of us could give a date. I was in my hospital bed very angry with my husband because I felt like he didn't care that I was in the hospital. I told myself, he didn't love me. I was sad, very sad and then I sought comfort from my ePartners and I wrote large on the white board that was facing my bed the verse from Isaiah 41:10. I read it every day as soon as I could. It soothed my heart.

I couldn't be with my family for Christmas, but I was still alive. I talked to my heavenly husband, confided in him, never doubted his faithfulness of bringing me home, but it was hard for me to accept that this would be done by HIS time not mine. I came back home on December 30. I was with my husband and children for New Years Eve. I was sad because I had seen no sign of affection from my husband since I was back. My husband saw my sadness so a few days later he came to talk with me to find out what was going on. I explained my feelings to him and you know what? My eyes lied to me. My husband cried, explaining to me that he was afraid of losing me, he said that he had prayed for me every day and that I didn't realize how hard it had been for him.

I was wrong. I looked at my circumstances and forgot to believe the Word. But my Heavenly Husband spoke to me through my husband that night.

Ministry Note: Had Annabella not been as physically weak, she wouldn't have explained her feelings in such a state, but she'd probably continue speaking only to the Lord her HH. However, GOD knew her EH (earthly husband) needed to hear her broken and weary heart in order for her EH to share his. Brides, don't make the mistake of trying this because when any of us have tried something similar—it blew up in our faces—setting us back a great deal in our restoration journeys.

Tell us HOW it happened, Annabella? Did your husband just walk in the front door?

My husband, who already has another apartment, promised to stay as long as possible with us until he could sign his resignation and move back in with the whole family. He sleeps here 6 days a week. In fact, he wears his wedding ring again.

Annabella, did you suspect or could you tell you were close to being restored?

Yes, I suspected when my husband took a half day off to see me and spend time with our son. He wanted to be with us. The simple request to be present with him was a sign to me that his heart was starting to turn.

Would you recommend any of our resources in particular that helped you, Annabella?

Online courses were the foundation. I think I read each course twice. Then the book How God Can and Will Restore Your Marriage, and then Wise Woman. The daily devotional is for me the key resource. It feels like our Heavenly Husband is whispering sweet words in our ears every morning.

Annabella, Do you have favorite Bible verses that you would like to pass on to women reading your Testimonies? Promises that He gave you?

In God have I put my trust; I will not be afraid what can man do unto me. Psalm 56:11

Thou wilt keep him in perfect peace, whose mind is stayed on Thee, because he trusteth in Thee. Isaiah 26:3

But there are many more.

Would you be interested in helping encourage other women, Annabella?

Yes

Either way, Annabella, what kind of encouragement would you like to leave women with, in conclusion?

I would say to have faith in God and not to look at your circumstances. I know it's not easy, but have faith in the Word above all else and keep your eyes on your Heavenly Husband. He will guide you step by step through this long and emotional journey.

Chapter 25

Alexi

"And I will give them one heart,
and put a new spirit within them.
And I will remove the heart of stone
from their flesh and give them a heart of flesh"
—Ezekiel 11:19

"The Desert was the School I Needed!"

Alexi, how did your Restoration Journey actually begin?

God says, "The king's heart is like a river controlled by the Lord, He directs it where He wants." Proverbs 21:1 and also promises that "I will give them a new will—an undivided heart—and plant a new spirit within them; I will remove their cold, stony heart and replace it with a warm heart of flesh. Ezekiel 11:19 and I want to say YES it is true!

I HAVE SO much joy and thanks to my Beloved Father because today I am here writing my long-dreamed and hoped-for testimony sharing all God did to restore my marriage! My husband returned home after I fell in love with my eternal Heavenly Husband, and God gave him a new heart!!

My testimony is more proof that NOTHING is impossible with God just as Erin said! Also, no one can stop the plans of God.

Well, I met my husband at the school where we were studying, and it took nine years and two months of dating and engagement until the big day of our wedding. I had an enviable marriage according to my friends, who thought it was great how my husband treated me, but over time I became arrogant, quarrelsome, jealous, contentious, and had all the faults of a foolish woman.

My first mistake was abandoning my first Love, I stopped going to church to stay at home controlling my husband. I wanted to be with him all the time, he had to do only my will. In short, I wanted to be the man of the house, everything had to be the way I wanted it. I fought with my husband all the time and always kicked him out any time I felt angry. I was very offensive with my words I flung at him. I always wanted to be right about everything. I took the place of my husband as the leader of our house.

I was totally foolish and ruined my marriage tearing it down with my own hands.

With all this harsh treatment, my husband started to become distant. Soon he was no longer the same man, but I never imagined that he had an OW. One day in the car I found a routine exam request that he had to do at his job and when I asked him why he hadn't told me, he replied that he had many other things that I didn't know.

Then a few days later, out of nowhere, my husband said that our marriage was over! He said that he couldn't give anymore, he was empty. He said that he hadn't loved me for a long time and that he just hadn't left yet because of our daughter. He said we didn't work anymore. That day my world fell apart— I didn't believe it was happening to me.

Like I'd been doing, I fought and insisted on knowing the reason. I told him I did not accept ending our marriage. I cried, screamed, begged, but nothing worked. This time he walked out on me (I didn't kick him out of the house), but as soon as he walked out the gate he turned around and yelled, "Do you really want to know the reason?! I've found someone who treats me like a man wants to be treated!!" When I heard about the existence of OW it was as if I had been stabbed in the chest. I begged him to stay with me and not to go. But he laughed and just walked away. For days I didn't eat, I just cried and lost a lot of weight in a very short time.

In a later conversation, we agreed that he would stay at home until we paid down some debts, and then he would go away but he was clear we were not a couple. This was a very difficult time for me to see my husband living a single life. Most nights he left and went out to meet the other woman, which ended up with me waiting up to fight with him. Until one day he arrived and we had an ugly fight that turned physical and verbally aggressive on both sides, and I kicked him out of our home.

For three days I begged him to come back and stay until the debts were paid off. When he came back, I didn't take the opportunity given to me, instead, I just fought and made him even angrier. While at the same time I kept crying and begging for love and asking him to come back to me. After another fight, he called my mom and told her to take me to her house or worse would happen. He said he didn't trust himself anymore!

When I arrived at my mother's, she told me to pray and ask God to save my family. I replied in a huff that I would not return to him even if God wanted me to! Needless to say, I paid a high price to get my husband back with words like that directed at God Himself!

I ended up staying with my mother for a little more than a month, and, it was during this period that a friend advised me to fight for my marriage and be a wise woman who builds her house. Those words stuck with me. My husband started sending me messages saying he missed me and told me that we had to go through all this to find out that he still loved me. One day he asked me out and as we were on our way back for him to drop me back, he asked me if I would stop staying at my mother's house and just come home. I did go home but I was the same, so things that were settling down at first, only got worse.

One day when I was coming back from a college class, I realized that he was no longer at home, he had packed and was gone. I cried a lot, called him a lot, making threats and sometimes declarations of my love for him. The more I pursued him, the more and aggressively he distanced himself from me and got even angrier. Next, I tried "tough love" saying that if he didn't want me anymore I didn't want him either. That blew up in my face when he put our house up for sale!

How did God change your situation, Alexi, as you sought Him wholeheartedly?

Six months passed, then God began to break me and put in my heart the desire to have my marriage and my family back together.

In an internet search for how to be a wise woman is when I found the book how God can and will restore your marriage. I read the book in three days with tears rolling down my face! It seemed that every word was written for me, as if Erin had been telling my story. Just then I started to realize my mistakes! Until then I only saw mistakes in my husband believing that he was guilty of everything. I did not realize that I was the biggest culprit in the destruction of my marriage.

My search for the restoration of my marriage started there. Instead of talking, I began praying, fasting, reading through the Bible, wanting more and more to have more intimacy with God, to learn to depend on Him for everything. God transformed me, I really knew God for the first time and I learned to depend on Him for everything, absolutely everything in my life.

I took all the RMI courses, some more than once! I fed myself spiritually with the morning devotionals, and read all the books from RMI on restoration. I asked God to help me apply the principles of the book. I confess that letting go was the most difficult when I needed the most help from my beloved God and I got it. I sincerely knew the love of God who was protective, merciful, and faithful, loving, caring, and glorious.

"And my God will supply all your needs according to His riches in glory in Christ Jesus." Philippians: 4:19. I really knew the love and power of God. I thank my Lord for everything He has done and continues to do in my life.

As the book teaches in the book how God Can and Will Restore Your Marriage, I first asked God for forgiveness for all my mistakes. I stopped fighting and stopped calling my husband. When I had the opportunity, I asked him for forgiveness for everything, and then personally, I agreed with the sale of our house. Agreed that it was one of the biggest reasons for our fights, and I handed it over to God that if it was His will that the house would be sold. I was shocked when I heard that everyone who came to see the house did not like it but it's an amazing house and I knew it was GOD who was in control, which gave me so much faith with everything else!

During this desert, I went through several trials that only God could have sustained and given me that strength to go through and still take care of my daughter without the help of her father. My desert lasted 2 years and 9 months and during that time my husband never helped me financially. I had to entirely support our daughter, let go of going to college (where I should never have been and where there is too much temptation), and got my dream job I'd been attending college to get without a degree!

I started to realize that my husband was also living in his desert when he sometimes sent a message asking for prayer. By this time, I was no longer quarrelsome and I treated my husband with affection when God gave me the opportunity to be close to him. Soon he started to treat me with affection again, then began to ask for favors when he started to get into debt. Even though he had a salary twice as much as mine, he needed financial help, asking for my help even to pay the rent for the apartment he lived in with the OW. As we were still married, I helped because my Lover strengthened me more and more.

What principles, from God's Word (or through our resources), Alexi, did the Lord teach you during this trial?

I learned that I was a totally foolish woman. I learned to begin to depend on God while letting go of my earthly husband.

I learned that I was in spiritual adultery, my EH (earthly husband) was above my HH (Heavenly Husband). It was through the book how God Can and Will Restore Your Marriage, that my search began, God directed me to this site and amazing ministry.

What were the most difficult times that God helped you through, Alexi?

The most difficult moments in the desert? Wow, there were several. I will not mention everything my husband did, uncovering him, because everyone going through the desert knows that it is not easy when our spouses are involved with someone else. We all know the pain of rejection and how horrible the humiliation is, but as a mom, what hurt the most was seeing my daughter suffering, missing her father when he called saying he was coming and then didn't show up. Then he called and didn't talk to her anymore because if he didn't come, she was not expecting it.

Another thing was to know (through relatives and friends) that he was so happy with OW (other woman), oh how it hurt. It's insane how heartless people can be when they knew of my broken heart but maybe they didn't because I stopped saying anything to anyone. Only God knew how I was doing. And as so many testimonies say, after he came home he told me he was never ever happy but did everything he could so he didn't feel the pain and emptiness.

The suffering is great, there are so many trials and attacks from the enemy that only God could help me through and I had to determine to never give up on the promises He had for my family, knowing His plans were much better than mine. There were so many difficult hours that He helped me through.

This desert was a great learning experience, God was molding me to be a new wife, woman, mother, and daughter. I surrendered myself totally to God and started to depend totally on Him. I didn't tell anyone that I was separated, nor that I was seeking restoration. It made me stronger spiritually when I fell in love with my HH and it didn't matter what my husband was doing anymore or if restoration would ever happen.

My family insisted that I should go on with my life and stop being silly and wait for my husband, that he had made his choice, and one day I agreed! God says to, "Agree with your adversary quickly"! (Matt. 5:25 KJV) but I didn't. But once I did, I agreed, I stopped getting so much opposition from everyone. It took reading Facing Divorce Again FOR ME TO GET IT!

Then after a conversation with my husband, I realized that he was also facing his desert, paying the price for his choices. He came over, asked me for forgiveness, he cried, and said that if I knew everything he had done, I would never forgive him. I said I did forgive him and we talked almost all night. I thought my desert was coming to an end, but God's timing is perfect and it is very different from ours.

He told me that he only had an OW to help him forget me and because he did not want to be alone, but that he was not happy, and that he had ruined his life. He said that he was ashamed and he couldn't face my parents or my family and just did not have the courage. We often think that our spouses are happy, but it is only a lie and deception by the enemy to steal our blessings and our peace.

Alexi, what was the "turning point" of your restoration?

When I rested in God after I met my HH. I also finally let go of my church and became His church, His bride. It was like walking out of the darkness and into the light.

Tell us HOW it happened, Alexi? Did your husband just walk in the front door? Alexi, did you suspect or could you tell you were close to being restored?

My husband never asked for a divorce, he said that we were only going to separate on paper when the house was sold, he had the key to our house and always showed up here. He often came to our house, and when he did, I treated him with affection, without wanting anything from him in return.

Soon my husband started showing up more often, he slept at home every other day (which caused a lot of arguing with the OW). Then he came home for lunch (so she wouldn't know) and started to come over more often. He came home to celebrate Christmas with us and didn't leave until New Year's Day.

I thought he was going back to her so I said "Bye, I'll see you soon" and gave him a big hug. Instead, he went over to get the rest of his stuff and has been here at home to the honor and glory of my Lord who restored and continues to restore my family! In February we traveled as a family to visit my family (including our daughter) and everything was wonderful. Everyone welcomed him with open arms! My husband has been home for more than a year. Yet, as Erin says the return of EH is not yet the end of our desert though the biggest battle has been won. Yet now I have the wisdom and relationship with my HH to remain firm in God who restored and who will complete the good work in me and my family.

My husband, who said that we no longer existed as a couple, is at home taking care of our family. After the OW learned that he was at home, she started calling my husband a lot and ended up getting a new cell phone because he was blocking her then this caused her to use the phone of his friends. Then, the OW started calling him on my cell phone and started saying she was pregnant. At first, I was a bit shaken, but God used the ePartner I had been encouraging, to give me promises to calm my heart. Every time I thought I couldn't take it anymore and wanted to give up, God spoke to me through His word and used people I was helping to strengthen me to continue.

Would you recommend any of our resources in particular that helped you, Alexi?

YES, for sure!! First, the book How God Can and Will Restore your Marriage. Get through all the courses because you will need them all. Wake up to the Daily Devotionals, and the Encourager.

Would you be interested in helping encourage other women, Alexi?

Yes

Either way, Alexi, what kind of encouragement would you like to leave women with, in conclusion?

What I have to say to everyone who is looking for the restoration of their families is that you must never give up on trusting Him. Agree with everyone to move on so you don't get opposition and move along your Restoration Journey quietly. Even if everything seems contrary to restoration, do not give up! If I were to look at what the human eyes could see, I would not be here with my husband and my daughter would not have a family. A family who, God loves and loves God and serves Him. Be patient and continue to wait for God's timing. God's will is good, perfect, and pleasant.

"For this reason, my brothers and sisters, be patient as you wait for the return of the Lord. Look! The farmer knows how to wait patiently for the land to produce vegetables and fruits. He cannot harvest a freshly planted seed. Instead, he waits for the early and late showers to nourish the soil." James 5:7, 8

"Look, we bless and honor the memory of those who persevered under hardship. Remember how Job endured and how the Lord orchestrated the triumph of his final circumstances as a grand display of His mercy and compassion." James 5:11.

Thank you my beloved HH thank you for everything YOU have done and continue to do in my life! Even though I am so flawed, You love me. I entered the desert a totally foolish woman and I am leaving shaped by the hands of God, this desert was the school I needed, not the universities of this world! I thank God for calling me to go through the desert with You, my HH

Chapter 26

Hande

"But prove yourselves doers of the word,
and not just hearers who deceive themselves."
—James 1:22

"No Longer an Adulteress, He is My First Love"

Hande, how did your Restoration Journey actually begin?

I had been married for a year and a half, my second marriage, and that's when it all started— right after the wedding. It's my fault. I was very jealous and controlling. Because I'd cheated in my first marriage I didn't trust anyone, so I'd open my husband's cell phone, scoured his emails, and always had a reason for fights. It was no big deal. I never took anything too seriously, but when my EH (earthly husband) wants to fight, my EH doesn't need much. He was also unemployed, and then, in addition to all my marriage issues, our finances started to get complicated. My EH was married before, so of course, he was being reduced to a loaf of bread as Erin says will happen. Partly had to do with when I had stopped working to be with my son (who was 2 years old at the time, now he is 4).

After many months of fights, he left for his mother's house and only came on weekends, and that's when physical attacks began. Verbal attacks were already common but I lashed out when he said things I didn't like. And him gone just made me more insecure, more jealous. That's when he can't take it and physically attacked me, after I attacked him. But that never came up when we went to see the church counselors. Everyone told me to report him and ask for a divorce, but something inside me said that I shouldn't do that.

So I searched for God, prayed, spent time in peace, but then it started all over again. Then it all made sense why. A few months later, my husband who said he was an atheist, came to accept Him as Lord, but we were still the same people, living in the same sin, so the fighting and abuse towards each other started all over again. Even worse than before.

How did God change your situation, Hande, as you sought Him wholeheartedly?

In April of that year, after crying for a few days, and asking and begging God to show me what to do, because I was already wanting a divorce, it happened. I was searching the internet for anything that would give me any hope and found RMI. I filled out the questionnaire, started to read the book How God can and will restore your marriage and wow, that helped me a lot and gave me hope! But I was focused only on my restoration, so when everything went well, I put the book and lessons aside. And soon, too soon I returned to being the quarrelsome, contentious, and a complete Pharisee... the same woman that I always was. And of course, the fights started again. I did everything wrong, including looking for psychological help, when I had already read that this was not a good idea. And I almost ended it all, attempting to take my own life.

What principles, from God's Word (or through our resources), Hande, did the Lord teach you during this trial?

In July after a horrible fight, where we spent 11 days apart, I went back to reading the RYM book. Then I answered the marriage assessment questionnaire again but this time the ministers insisted I go through Finding the Abundant Life. Soon after I started the lessons, my EH contacted me, we made up, but I didn't trust God alone (since I hadn't really embraced my HH). So I still went to 2 more sessions with psychologists taking my EH. During the second session, I said a lot of bad things, and this time I almost destroyed everything, me, and him. After what I said, he hated me. He said he never wanted to see me again, and he wanted a divorce. He said nothing would ever change and that he didn't want this life for himself. I was devastated, but this time I turned my focus on doing the lessons and reading the FAL book. Two days later, I read a testimony that looked a lot like my story, and God took the blindfold off my eyes. I cried a lot, and suddenly I understood everything. That I was to blame for everything, and that I did not deserve the forgiveness of my husband or God. I felt dirty, ashamed but that was about to change.

What were the most difficult times that God helped you through, Hande?

I asked God for forgiveness and on the same day, I forgave my husband. Then God provided the opportunity to ask my EH's forgiveness. I said I knew he wasn't going to forgive me because I didn't deserve it. That I would give him a divorce because I was to blame for everything. He said he forgave me. That he loved me. This happened on a Sunday.

As he spends the week working with his father, he stays at his parent's home during the week. He left on Sunday, and it was the most difficult week but God was changing me. I started to obey, to follow the principles of silence. And focused on fixing some things wrong here at home. But during the week GOD hardened his heart, and I then told God that I accepted whatever came from Him. I read Facing Divorce again (one of the best books so far). I told Him that if that was his will, I would accept it and that because in His eyes this was adultery, I honestly wanted out.

The next weekend he came home to give me some money, but he said he didn't want to stay. That he was disgusted, and he didn't want to look at me. He said he had forgiven me, but he didn't want me anymore. I obeyed that principle of agreeing with him on everything and even adding more to his list. He said a lot of things about me, and I agreed. The truth is, everything he said was true, and I hadn't really recognized it until that week.

Hande, what was the "turning point" of your restoration?

The turning point of our restoration was that day after he said all these things and I agreed and I didn't defend myself, as I'd always done before. That night he ended up sleeping here. On Sunday I continued following the entire set of principles, step by step of the book and doing my FAL lessons. I also started to read the Psalms and Proverbs and began to tithe again, this time to my storehouse.

The turning point of my life was finding my True Love, my HH. Understanding I was the adulteress because of my unfaithfulness to Him.

Tell us HOW it happened, Hande? Did your husband just walk in the front door? Hande, did you suspect or could you tell you were close to being restored?

It took less than 15 days, two weeks exactly when everything changed. All. Now 5 months later I can say that I have a dream marriage, which seems impossible because I am living in adultery but I am no longer my HH adulteress because He is my first love.

My kids are obeying us now because I'm obedient to the Lord and submissive to my EH. Even my 16-year-old daughter, who was very rebellious, changed in an instant watching my example. My oldest daughter is reconciled to the Lord and then with her husband and began going to church. My home has peace for the first time ever. Because I am submissive to everything each day my EH has been more loving, caring, kind. He went back to wearing a wedding ring. (He had thrown it away, then he took me to buy new rings).

We had already asked for forgiveness for everything from each other, but there are many nights we have cried together, but this time with happiness, because we never imagined that we would be like this. Today we spent hours together, talking, laughing. I don't need to charge anything because my EH does things without me saying a word. I'm still hoping that one day he will become my spiritual leader. Right now I'm on Moving Mountains and even though it appears to be about finances, the principles cover everything seemingly impossible.

Would you recommend any of our resources in particular that helped you, Hande?

I recommend everything. Read the book God can and will restore your marriage. Take the courses. ALL of them. Read the Devotionals. Start reading the Bible (Psalms and Proverbs) and then begin reading through the entire bible. Be sure to follow everything in each of these materials. Do what it says. Because it's all true. And you will know the truth, and the truth will set you free. John 8:32

Would you be interested in helping encourage other women, Hande?

Yes

Either way, Hande, what kind of encouragement would you like to leave women with, in conclusion?

Trust God. Obey the principles of His Word, and as the Psalmist says,

"Trust in the Lord with all your heart and do not lean on your own understanding. In all your ways acknowledge Him, and He will make your paths straight." Proverbs 3:5–6

Don't give up on your family. Stop fighting with your spouse, but never stop fighting for your family, and for the soul of your husband. The reward is worth every effort. Praise God for this ministry, for Erin's life, and for all that are part of this ministry ... I hope that soon, I too, will be a part of your team and help bring hope to other women and men. I already talk about the site to everyone. Everyone! And there are already 4 people who are taking the courses, almost a dozen others reading the book that I bought and gave to them. Praise the Lord!!!

Chapter 27

Pinar

"Stop striving and know that I am God;
I will be exalted among the nations,
I will be exalted on the earth."
—Psalm 46:10

"The Freedom to Let Go"

Pinar, how did your Restoration Journey actually begin?

We had been married for 20 years, we have 2 children and this is the fourth time that we have been through a crisis in marriage. Each of the previous three times God restored our marriage, but I continued to build my house on sinking sand. I was a foolish woman, and never trusted the restoration that God had done. So I snooped on his phone, in his pockets, everything I could. In this fourth crisis, due to me neglecting my time with the Lord completely, I became a feisty, jealous woman and kept my EH (earthly husband) more and more away from me.

In one of my daily inspections, I discovered a message on his cell phone where I realized that my EH was again in adultery. I made the mistake of confronting him about it and telling countless people how unfaithful my EH was. Because I attacked him openly and cornered him, he left the house for a week.

After that period he returned home saying he was sorry, but soon after I persisted in being a foolish woman I discovered that he was still in contact with OW "other women." I was devastated and confronted him again. He then said that he was confused and that he wanted 3 months' time, but that he would remain living at home. He lived at home, but it was like he didn't live there at all, he didn't have a time set to arrive, and some nights he slept God knows where. During this period, I had already found another marriage help site, I started pursing him as the ministry suggested...sending messages, controlling his schedules, which made him want to get even further away from me.

After 10 days of making everything worse, I discovered RMI and its wonderful principles. I read the book How God can and will restore your marriage in just 2 days and immediately started putting what I was learning into practice. I realized how much I had been wrong during all my many years of marriage and started to believe that God would restore my marriage and that now it would be definitive, because I would build my house on the Rock. I started to hope again.

How did God change your situation, Pinar, as you sought Him wholeheartedly?

I read and reread the book How God can and will restore your marriage several times, then I started taking courses online, watching the encouraging videos day after day. Journaling really made everything more clear. I started trusting God to restore my marriage, with all my heart, I truly trusted my life in His hands. I recognized my mistakes and asked for forgiveness from God and my EH. Since then, I have experienced a relationship with my HH (Heavenly Husband) that I have never experienced in my life, despite being born in a Christian home. At the beginning of my journey, I felt anxious, suffocated, with no hope of life. As I was SG (seeking God) and learning more and more by using all the resources offered by RMI, my heart was filled with peace. A peace that surpasses all understanding.

What principles, from God's Word (or through our resources), Pinar, did the Lord teach you during this trial?

I thank God for introducing me to RMI because it helped me when I needed it most when I was at rock bottom. With the resources of RMI, I learned precious principles that I will carry throughout my life. One of the essential points was to realize that I also contributed to the situation my marriage was in. I realized the need to let go of my EH because my attitudes only helped to keep him away. I stopped sending messages, controlling his schedules, and delivered them to my HH. I started to apply the principle of Winning Without Words and Kindness on the Tongue, I didn't complain and ask my EH for anything. Daily I asked God for wisdom and asked Him to fill my heart with love for my EH so that I could forgive him daily.

Regardless of the time he came home or slept elsewhere, no matter when he arrived, even if it was the next day, I greeted him kindly with love and care. We continued to have intimacy and at the beginning, I asked God daily to turn his heart towards me, the woman of his youth. "May your source be blessed! Rejoice with the wife of your youth. Loving gazelle, graceful doe; may your wife's breasts always fill you with pleasure, and her caresses always make you drunk." Proverbs 5: 18,19 NIV.

Another principle that gave me peace of mind was the fasting of social networks, no longer following the gossip of social networks. It was so liberating.

I started to apply the principle of tithing because I attended church, but I was not faithful in tithe, I just gave an offering. Still, I didn't see any fruits until I let go of my church who'd never fed me spiritually with the truth, and joined RF tithing to my storehouse. This was the moment I saw things clearly like a veil was lifted from my eyes.

For me, the biggest principle I learned was the need for my HH to be in first place. That principle set me free. How wonderful it is to pour ourselves into the arms of our HH, with the conviction that He is taking care of everything, including my two children, because He is a kind and loving Heavenly Father.

I used workers@home to help organize my time so that I could spend more and more time with Him, fasting, and praying constantly. Every day I felt more desire and yearned to be with Him. "In the same way, women, submit to your husbands, so that if some of them do not obey the word, they may be won without words, by the procedure of your wife." 1 Peter 3:1 NIV

What were the most difficult times that God helped you through, Pinar?

The most difficult moment was when my EH spent the night with the OW on our wedding anniversary, but my HH blessed me in such a way that I managed to get through this day more strengthened and more in love with Him. I had in mind the principle that it was not my EH that he was rejecting me but that God took him away from me to fulfill a purpose in my life.

"If an enemy insulted me, I could take it; if an opponent stood up against me, I could defend myself; but soon you, my colleague, my companion, my close friend, you, with whom I shared a pleasant fellowship as we went with the festive crowd to the house of God!" Psalms 55:12-14 NIV

"All my close friends hate me; those whom I love have turned against me." Job 19:19 NIV

"The king's heart is like channels of water in the hand of the LORD; He turns it wherever He wishes." Proverbs 21:1

Pinar, what was the "turning point" of your restoration?

The turning point of my restoration was when I read the chapter "The Freedom to Let Go" and truly understood this principle. Until that moment I hadn't yet stopped sending messages, controlling the time of his arrival at home, but when I studied this lesson I realized that I was not applying this principle correctly, because my EH was still the first one in my thoughts and in my heart. When I realized that I was being unfaithful to my HH, I started praying and asking the Lord to empty my heart of everything that was taking His place. I understood that I needed to stop praying for my EH because my EH was in control of everything. It was very difficult to stop praying for him, at first I felt a void, but soon after, that void was filled by my beloved HH. How lovely!! The more I looked for Him, the more He filled me with His love and brought peace to my heart. It was then that my EH started to act differently, started to show regret, and treat me with love.

Tell us HOW it happened, Pinar? Did your husband just walk in the front door? Pinar, did you suspect or could you tell you were close to being restored?

My EH again said that he loved me and wanted to be with me. The more I looked for my HH, the more my EH turned his heart towards me. I felt that my restoration was near. It was exactly 4 months after this crisis when my EH began coming home saying every day that I was the best mother and wife there is and that he even wanted to have another child with me. I was scared because having a third child had never crossed his mind. He completed by saying that I was special and pleasant, different from any OW. I realized then that my beloved GOD was restoring my marriage. I know that we still have a journey ahead of us and that I will still be well tested, but I am firm in my relationship with my EH and I will enjoy every minute in His presence. "You will not fear bad news; your heart is steadfast, confident in the Lord."

Would you recommend any of our resources in particular that helped you, Pinar?

I would recommend the books How God Can and Will Restore Your Marriage and A Wise Woman, your courses and videos.

Would you be interested in helping encourage other women, Pinar?

Yesssss

Either way, Pinar, what kind of encouragement would you like to leave women with, in conclusion?

Beloved, follow the principles taught in the resources of RMI, SG with all your heart, meditate on His Word, fast, truly give your lives in His hands. Believe me, don't lose hope, even though your situation may seem like you have no hope. Do not listen to the enemy's voice. When the enemy is trying to talk to you, meditate on God's promises, have those promises engraved on your heart. Do not be afraid, because our wonderful God knows us by name, knows all our needs, and is in control of everything.

See your situation with spiritual eyes. In the meantime, let your heart be flooded with the peace and love of our dear and beloved Heavenly Husband. "Stop fighting! Know that I am God! I will be exalted among the nations, I will be exalted on earth." Psalm 46:10 NIV

"Wait on the Lord. Be strong! Courage! Wait on the Lord." Ps 27:14

"For nothing is impossible with God." Luke 1:37

"Against all hope, in hope, he believed." Romans 4:18

"For everything there is an occasion and a time for every purpose under heaven." Ecclesiastes 3:1

"As for the Lord, His eyes go over the whole earth, to show himself strong towards those whose heart is perfect towards Him." 2 Corinthians 16:9

Chapter 28

Josie

"Behold, the Lord's hand is not so short
That it cannot save;
Nor is His ear so dull
That it cannot hear."
—Isaiah 59:1

"Such Pain and Shock that I Wanted to Die"

Josie, how did your Restoration Journey actually begin?

My restoration journey started when I asked my husband for a divorce at the end of April. The previous 6 years had been quite challenging for us. We married in 2000, as believers but carrying a lot of baggage from the world. We had a good marriage but it was never what either of us had dreamt of. I was unsubmissive, independent, argumentative, proud, passive aggressive, etc. My husband responded with anger and irritability. I didn't realize how my behavior caused so many of our problems and is what led to me feeling unloved.

Also, although I knew the Lord as my Savior, I hadn't fully submitted myself to His will. At the end of 2013, I became rebellious against God after a big fight where my EH (earthly husband) told me to find someone to do all the things I was complaining about. I used that as an excuse to accept the advances from my manager at work and soon began an adulterous relationship. I was mean, angry, and unloving toward my husband at that time and he suffered a lot of pain while trying to save our precious family.

I reluctantly agreed to stop contact with my manager after just a few months and moved to a different work location. We tried to move forward with our family and marriage but I still hadn't learned how to be a Godly wife. I grew tired of my EH's pain being directed at me through his anger and I moved out in August two years later. I soon started to date another manager behind my husband's back and he found out again. During that time, I was depressed and full of anxiety. I had no peace and I knew I needed the Lord's help.

Finally, around June about a year after that, I cried out to Him to help me. I had just filed divorce because I thought that's what I had to do but didn't feel any peace about it. That same month, God removed the OM (other man) by showing me the truth about him. I was in such turmoil that I cried out to the Lord again. This time, I heard Him tell me "Humble yourself and go back to your husband!" A few days later, I was having a panic attack and asked my husband to come over. I confessed everything and asked if he'd be willing to take me back. Although he'd been hurt so much, he agreed!! I was so relieved and thought we could put all the past behind us.

Well, neither of us changed much and we just kept making the same mistakes. Fast forward to April of last year when I asked him for a divorce again. Once again, I fooled myself into thinking that was the answer to all my pain. Well, I was soooo wrong! My husband tried desperately to change my mind but I would not listen. I felt that nothing would change and I made sure the kids knew he was being emotionally abusive. Of course, I was blind to my own abuse of him and all I'd put him and the kids through. The Lord even tried to warn me by saying "Don't take this too far!" God KNEW I really didn't want a divorce but I was desperate for relief.

My EH gave up trying to convince me and decided to give me what I asked for so around our 20th year anniversary in May he agreed to give me an immediate release from the marriage. He was serious. I wasn't and was just being prideful so I went along. He'd started to talk about dating but I convinced myself that he wouldn't do that until AFTER the divorce. I was so prideful!!

Just a couple of weeks later, in June, I began to suspect he was seeing someone and looked through his things to confirm. I confronted him and things just went downhill from there. From then on, it was in my face. I was convicted by the Lord instantly once I realized my foolishness and I tried desperately to make things right. I asked for forgiveness and begged my husband to end things with the OW (other woman) and save the marriage. He refused and, really, who can blame him? He was so distraught by everything I'd put him through that he just gave up on everything: God, our marriage, our kids, and even his own safety and wellbeing.

How did God change your situation, Josie, as you sought Him wholeheartedly?

From the very point that I was convicted for my foolishness, I knew God wanted to save my marriage. I KNEW that He had a plan and He needed me to trust Him. I just had no idea how to go about doing that. I had always made God fit into my plans so I didn't know how to surrender my will to Him. It was very difficult in the beginning. I was so heartbroken that I could not eat or sleep. I lost 30 pounds in a matter of days. I did almost everything wrong in the beginning: I talked to everyone who would listen hoping they had answers for me, purchased a psychology-based Christian marriage program, purchased a couple of astrology-based books, studied astral charts, pursued, begged, and cried to my husband to take me back, confronted the OW, forced myself back into our bedroom after I'd moved out against my husband's wishes, snooped through his things, played holy spirit by telling him how he was sinning, etc. I soon started to realize that none of those things were helping so I, finally, turned to God completely.

I asked Him "What is the Key to restoring my marriage?" and He answered "Unconditional love." I began to apply this principle and started to see immediate results. My EH was being kind to me despite all we were going through. We started being intimate although he was torn about doing that with me while being involved with the OW.

I started following other restoration ministries but I felt something was missing. I asked the Lord to send me some practical biblically-based advice that I could apply to my situation and help me change. The Lord had been showing me so much about myself and the type of wife I'd been. I was torn over my sin but full of hope. I was determined to submit myself to His will and to be obedient no matter what it took. Then, in the beginning of November, I heard about the RYM book through another ministry. I bought it and began to read it right away. The first chapter had me in tears of gratefulness to my Lord for answering my prayer. THIS was the answer!! THIS is what I'd been looking for. This book was talking to me. It was written about me. In reading the book, I found out about the lessons online which I began in November.

What principles, from God's Word (or through our resources), Josie, did the Lord teach you during this trial?

The Lord showed me that I had been the foolish woman who tore her house down with her own hands. I had been blinded by my anger, resentment, bitterness, and unforgiveness over past hurts. I was not a good wife although I always thought I was. My heart broke for my husband and our children and all I put them through. I was such a hypocritical Pharisee! I thought I was the spiritual authority but my self-righteousness was as filthy rags. I knew nothing about being a Godly wife. But GOD! In His mercy, grace, and love, He allowed me to become His Son's bride. My Heavenly Husband taught me about having a quiet and gentle spirit, winning my EH without words, unconditional love, patience, forgiveness, submission, agreeing with my adversary quickly, leaving the church, not playing holy spirit, stepping out of the way of sinners, intimacy while married, wearing my wedding rings, not pursuing my husband, running to my Beloved whenever I was hurting or to celebrate what He was doing, allowing my HH to be my Defender, letting go of my need to be understood which led to contentiousness, spending tons of time with Him in my prayer room, allowing myself to be loved by Him, letting Him become my Heavenly Husband, and so much more! My Heavenly Husband would speak to me about something and then I would do a lesson that would reinforce exactly what He'd said.

What were the most difficult times that God helped you through, Josie?

The most difficult times in my journey were in the beginning when I was in such pain and shock that I wanted to die. The Lord spared my life by placing a very good friend in my path to speak life and hope into me. Another was living with my EH while he was seeing the OW. He'd moved out just one month after starting to see her but spent the majority of his time at home with me and the kids. Just one month later, he moved back in. It was very painful being aware of everything: when they spoke on the phone, when they texted, when he left to go see her, when he came back. Since we were still in our marital bedroom, I would see him when he got back from her house and got in bed with me to cuddle. The most difficult was being intimate knowing what he was doing but I trusted the Lord who'd told me from the beginning that it was His will.

I'd asked what was the purpose of wanting me to be intim; knowing how difficult it was for me. My HH told me that know how He feels when we (His Bride) are lukewarm. V foot in the world and another in heaven. We have been adulterous and have hurt Him immensely, yet He did not leave us. Instead, He showed us His unconditional love and welcomed us back every time we returned.

He wanted me to see and truly understand what I had done. This was not punishment but an opportunity for the eyes of my understanding to be opened; an opportunity to experience what He goes through every day. I felt so humbled and grateful! I put aside the thoughts of the OW and just focused on the gift my HH had given me to love my husband and show him the Lord's love. Thank You, my Love!!

Josie, what was the "turning point" of your restoration?

The turning point of our restoration was when I started to apply the principles I learned through RMI. As I mentioned, I started the lessons on November 9th. I had learned to pray scripture and prayed some very specific prayers over my situation. My HH is so good to me that He answered so many of my prayers the way I'd asked Him to and I believe it's because it was His will and His Word coming back to Him. On November 27th, I went out of town for a wedding and while away the enemy attacked me with thoughts of what my EH might be up to. I decided enough was enough and I just let it go. I made a decision to truly surrender and accept God's will.

I want to give my Heavenly Husband all the praise and all the glory He deserves for healing me emotionally and mentally. Many years ago, I was diagnosed with depression and anxiety disorder. None of the counseling or meds ever worked, the ONLY thing that ever worked for me was surrendering to my Lord. Yet, because of my frequent backsliding, I continued to struggle with these things whenever life got tough during the times I wasn't walking with Him. This is exactly what happened when my RJ started in the Summer of 2020. I'd asked my EH for a divorce and refused to listen to him as he tried desperately to save our precious marriage. I also ignored the Him as He tried to warn me of my huge mistake. I was finally broken down once I found out about the OW and the Lord convicted me of my rebellious ways. I knew He had a plan and wanted me to surrender but I had no clue how to do that! I responded the same way I had in the past - through depression and extreme anxiety. I was so used to fixing things on my own without the Lord's help that I tried to do the same and things would only get worse. I was battling suicidal thoughts and had panic attacks. I tried counseling but the counselor told me I didn't need to be there because I kept talking about the Lord, lol. This was Christian counseling!! But she said they focus on the clinical aspect. I finally started to get everything my Lord had been speaking to me and I started to lean in to Him. I knew medication was not the answer, only my Lord could help me. This was a spiritual battle that was attacking my thoughts and my emotions. The enemy was doing his best to kill me, destroy my marriage and family, and steal our peace and joy. But my GOD is greater than the one who is in the world. My Beloved taught me how to surrender my will to His, how to spend time in prayer, how to pray scriptures over everything, how to battle in the spirit, how to trust Him only, how to praise Him when I was angry and just felt like crying, etc. He led me to RMI and He healed me completely. I have such peace and joy now and I laugh so much more than I cry (I cried so much during the hardest months than I knew was humanly possible!). He is my EVERYTHING and I love Him with all that is in me.

"She is clothed with strength and dignity, and she laughs without fear of the future." Proverbs 31:25

"Come to me, all you who are weary and burdened, and I will give you rest. Take my yoke upon you and learn from me, for I am gentle and humble in heart, and you will find rest for your souls. For my yoke is easy and my burden is light." Matthew 11:28-30

"This is what the Lord says: 'Restrain your voice from weeping and your eyes from tears, for your work will be rewarded,' declares the Lord. 'They will return from the land of the enemy.'" Jeremiah 31:16

Tell us HOW it happened, Josie? Did your husband just walk in the front door?

The day after I returned home (Nov 30th), my EH had a talk with me. He said he'd ended things with the OW and that he'd lost interest in her because of me. He said he loves me this way (with the changes my HH made). I thought he would say he'd like to try again and ask for forgiveness for hurting me.

Instead, there was a lot of anger from him. He said he felt it was all a trick and that I would just hurt him again so he still needed to move forward with the divorce. I simply replied, "okay". He said other hurtful things and that he would just find another girl. Again, I said "okay". He couldn't believe I was so calm and asked what was I doing? I simply said that I was not willing to try to manipulate him or try to make him be with me if he didn't want to. I would not stand in his way and if he wanted a divorce, I would not fight it. I said I understood why he felt the way he did and I was sorry.

I also said that even if he found someone else, I would continue to love him. For some reason, however, I also said that if he started dating someone, I wouldn't be intimate with him because I needed to be safe. This shocked him and I think it may have served to show that I wouldn't use sex to manipulate him (he'd made several comments about me being intimate with him to try to win him back). Honestly, I would have continued to be intimate if he still wanted me. Later, he came to me, hugged me and said he wouldn't date anyone else and that he is just afraid of getting hurt.

Josie, did you suspect or could you tell you were close to being restored?

I could tell we were close because he was at home more often and for longer times. When he did leave, he would leave a lot later than usual and come back much earlier. Then, he stayed home for the first Friday since our journey began and I knew something was happening. This was one of the many specific prayers I mentioned; that the first Friday he stayed home would serve as a sign that his heart was turning back to me. I'd also asked my HH to prepare me for what's coming so I felt it in my spirit and He also gave me several dreams back to back.

Would you recommend any of our resources in particular that helped you, Josie?

I strongly recommend the RYM book and the courses. They were very impactful for me and I'm still working through them. I plan to finish them all and continue the other lessons available. I'm also looking forward to reading the Wise Woman and Workers at Home. I also strongly recommend the Testimony books and the Encourager blog. Those kept me going during the most difficult times. It was so encouraging to know that I was not alone and that nothing is impossible with God. If He could turn around so many other marriages, then why not mine?

Writing scripture on 3x5 cards really helped me and I still read them often. I also highlighted a lot of verses in my Bible. Praying scripture was a life-changer for me and so powerful! Finally, the Encourager Videos were a tremendous help in putting concepts together for me. I felt like Erin was in my living room talking to me. She has become like my Spiritual Mother.

Do you have favorite Bible verses that you would like to pass on to women reading your Testimonies Josie? Promises that He gave you?

"Blessed is she who has believed that the Lord would fulfill His promises to her!" Luke 1:45

"Wives, in the same way submit yourselves to your own husbands so that, if any of them do not believe the word, they may be won over without words by the behavior of their wives." 1 Peter 3:1

"... in reverent fear of God submit yourselves to your masters, not only to those who are good and considerate, but also to those who are harsh. For it is commendable if someone bears up under the pain of unjust suffering because they are conscious of God. But how is it to your credit if you receive a beating for doing wrong and endure it? But if you suffer for doing good and you endure it, this is commendable before God." 1 Peter 2:18-20

"Blessed is the one who does not walk in step with the wicked or stand in the way that sinners take or sit in the company of mockers." Psalm 1:1

"Forget the former things; do not dwell on the past. See, I am doing a new thing! Now it springs up; do you not perceive it? I am making a way in the wilderness and streams in the wasteland." Isaiah 43:18-19

"Surely the arm of the LORD is not too short to save, nor his ear too dull to hear." Isaiah 59:1

All of Psalm 37

Would you be interested in helping encourage other women, Josie?

Yes ;)

Either way, Josie, what kind of encouragement would you like to leave women with, in conclusion?

Dear Brides, do you know that our Lord is no respecter of persons? That means that what He has done for me, He will do for you. He wants your whole heart so surrender to Him completely and then trust Him for the outcome. He knows what He's doing and He wants nothing but the absolute best for you. Make up your mind to be radically obedient to Him not caring what anyone else may think or say about you. Learn to pray His Word in every instance and you will see your faith grow and the enemy flee! His Word says that "God is not a man that He should lie; neither the son of man, that he should repent" (Num 23:19) and that He "watch[es] over [His] word to perform it" (Jer 1:12). That means you can trust every Word that comes out of His mouth. Remember: God wins!

Chapter 29

Alyssa

"There is an appointed time for everything.
And there is a time for every matter under heaven"
—Ecclesiastes 3:1

"Pride Took Me Straight to the Desert"

Alyssa, how did your Restoration Journey actually begin?

This started when we'd been married for 10 years with 2 beautiful daughters. I believe that, like everyone who arrives at the RMI seeking help to cross this desert, I was a fool who destroyed my own home. I was contentious, proud, I wanted my own way without caring whether it would hurt my husband or not. I had a nice job, which generated a very good income, and several times I threw that in my husband's face that I earned as much as he did and that he should do as much in our home as I did. I didn't think it was "fair" for me to have to take care of the house alone since I put as much money in the house and worked the same 8 hours as he did. Anyway, to sum up, I was not wise enough and my pride took me straight to the desert. My husband became more and more distant until he told me that he would leave and move out of the house as soon as he found a place to stay. My pride was so huge that I didn't even believe he was serious about what he said he'd do because several times he threatened that and I got around the situation after I'd made promises after more promises that I would improve, but it didn't last long and I was the same as always...

A few days later, I lost my job and deep down I thought it would be great because knowing him as I knew him I was sure that he would never abandon me if I was out of a job. As the days went by and he didn't leave the house, I became more and more confident that he would give up on the idea of moving out. But I was wrong, one day he came home saying he was packing and left that morning. I was speechless.

Ashamed, I went through it all alone, without talking to my parents, I told them. I didn't want them to be angry with my husband when he returned. I decided to tell only the people who, like me, believed that God could change my situation and restore my marriage. I didn't need or want advice from anyone who thought differently from the Word of God. He hates divorce. So I surrounded myself with whoever believed that and gave me the strength to continue my battle. Finally, I was no longer a fool but becoming wise.

How did God change your situation, Alyssa, as you sought Him wholeheartedly?

That day, completely lost, I fell at the Lord's feet. I could see that he left my life, not because of a lack of love, but because I had indeed become a horrible wife. Selfish, self-centered, self-sufficient, and so on. So first I asked God for forgiveness for being such a fool and for building my home in the sand. Sometimes my husband begged me for attention and said exactly what I should do to save my marriage ... and yet, I ignored his pleas ... how silly ... afterward, I went onto your website ordering everything from your bookstore, requested prayer, and asked them to intercede for my family. I thought that the more people praying for me, the quicker the restoration would be ... check it out! I reached out and posted a prayer request to more than 150 sites to order that God would be merciful to me. But very soon I realized how foolish I was. My husband had already said that I had to change my ways of being who no one wanted to be around, but I didn't listen to him. So God made me realize this the moment he stepped out of the house. In my first prayers, I asked God to mold me and to help me be a woman after His heart. The day I found the RMI website, after ordering everything, I started the courses and devoured the Book How God can and will restore your marriage in less than 2 days.

What principles, from God's Word (or through our resources), Alyssa, did the Lord teach you during this trial?

I started to put the book's principles into practice and I stuck to the following passage: "Everything has its own time, and there is time for the whole purpose under heaven." Ecclesiastes 3:1. After a few months of suffering - which is expected for everyone who goes through this situation - God placed in my heart that everything was a matter of time. I had that very clear in my head. That, in a matter of time, he would return, regardless of the direction our lives had taken. When I understood the principle of "letting go" and resting in God, things became less painful to cross my desert. The pain was gone when I journaled through most of finding my abundant life like so many restored testimonies I read also said.

What were the most difficult times that God helped you through, Alyssa?

At first, I looked for information on social networks, but after seeing something that hurt me, I stopped following it. I was sure that he had started a friendship on the social network with someone he was dating. I was sure they were having a relationship even though - in all the time we were apart - he never posted a photo of the two of them together. Even after I fasted social media, I ended up finding out that he started taking her to parties at his brother's house - which confirmed my certainty even more ... but none of that shook my faith. It just motivated me to discover my own Lover who would transform me with His love.

God is the Creator of the family, He more than anyone was interested in restoring it. And I knew that God was there with me, supporting and comforting me. For several nights I felt the presence of God in the midst of my tears. In the same month, he moved from the city we lived in because he had also lost his job. He stayed at his brother's, uncle's, mother's, aunt's house ... he jumped from house to house, without having a fixed home but never did I hear he was living with the OW so each time I was grateful He was working.

Alyssa, what was the "turning point" of your restoration?

Most of the few meetings with my husband were cold, he hardly spoke to me, he had a cold hard look in his eyes, but at the same time, he looked sad. I saw in his eyes that he was trying to give me an impression of something that was a lie. Even so, every time I knew I would see him, I asked God for wisdom to be kind regardless of what I saw or what he said. Sometimes I found some excuse for him to talk to me on the phone ... But as time passed and nothing improved, I realized I wasn't trusting God to restore my marriage and again I was in adultery not putting my HH first, so I gradually let it go and agreed with family and friends to move on. I had no intention of finding a new man because by that time I had my HH.

I believe that at that point I started to rest in the Lord. Enjoy my time with him and came to the point I really questioned if I wanted to be restored or devote my life to the Lord. "To those who are married, here's my command (to be clear, this isn't merely my opinion; it comes from the teaching of the Lord Jesus): it is not right for a wife to leave her husband. If she does, she must either remain single or reconcile with her husband, but she should not marry someone else. Likewise, the husband should not divorce his wife. The woman who is unmarried, and the virgin, is concerned about the things of the Lord, that she may be holy both in body and spirit; but one who is married is concerned about the things of the world, how she may please her husband" 1 Corinthians 7:10-11, 34

What's amazing is that even without a job, I never lacked anything at home. God always touched my parents' hearts or even strangers to provide what was missing, without even mentioning anything to anyone.

Tell us HOW it happened, Alyssa? Did your husband just walk in the front door? Alyssa, did you suspect or could you tell you were close to being restored?

My youngest daughter became very ill. When I was on my way to the hospital, out of nowhere my husband contacted me by a message asking about the children and I told him where I was going. Worried he asked me to call him to say what she had, he ended the message by asking if I wanted him to come to my house to help me with her. I did not answer. I asked God for wisdom to answer the message. When I did text back, he called me from a very noisy place (it sounded like a party), he said he would call me in 20 minutes from a quieter place. When I spoke to him, I replied that there was no need for him to come home, but that any help would be welcomed. He did come and stayed for a few days, but I saw him on his cell phone while he was in the bathroom, and heard him say "Good morning" and could tell it was the OW. I got away quickly to speak to my Lover and soon felt calm, but more than ever I was not interested in restoration.

In the bathroom, I asked God for strength so that this onslaught of anything wicked wouldn't affect me anymore. And thanks to Him, it didn't any more! From then on, visits each weekend became more frequent when he'd come during the week.

With little money, picking up the kids, and going back to the city where he lived was expensive, so he started to come and stay at our house all weekend long. We went for walks, we spent family moments that we hadn't had in a long time.

After a few months of being a family, me with my Lover and clearly, his lover was gone, we agreed to move to the city where we live today. We went together to choose the best home for us. At our youngest daughter's birthday party, he started to introduce me as his wife and since then, to the honor and glory of the Lord, our marriage has been fully restored.

Would you recommend any of our resources in particular that helped you, Alyssa?

Yes of course. Everything I've mentioned.

Would you be interested in helping encourage other women, Alyssa?

Yes, of course.

Either way, Alyssa, what kind of encouragement would you like to leave women with, in conclusion?

Don't give up on your family. Keep your focus on God, not circumstances. God will honor every tear, every knee on the floor because He is with you! Fall in love with your HH and save yourself all the pain that comes with being rejected. Let go, move on and find yourself an abundant life.

Chapter 30

Nazik

"The heart is more deceitful than all else
And is desperately sick;
Who can understand it?"
—Jeremiah 17:9

"Involved with Random Guy and am Left with So Much Pain from Regret"

Nazik, how did your Restoration Journey actually begin?

My restoration journey started in September three years ago. My EH (earth husband) and I had just married in March of that year. We were already partners and we lived together for two years without making our union official. From the beginning of our relationship, the Lord used several people who confirmed that our union was the will of our Beloved. However, my EH and I were encouraged by everyone to live together before we married, and today I am sure that the crisis we faced was due to this gigantic disobedience to the voice of the Lord.

I come from a home without any marriage structure. My parents broke up when I was seven and I never had any example of a Godly marriage. Quite the opposite, after the separation of my parents, I went to live with my father and he raised me to be independent and self-sufficient. So you can already imagine that I would not know at all how to be a good wife after having my dad live with many women coming and going.

My husband also comes from a home without a spiritual foundation. His father got involved with several other women besides his mother and even had a daughter outside of marriage during the period when we lived together. So my EH decided to live together without any conditions for that.

Everything escalated after a big fight, when my EH told me that if he had to make a decision that day and decided what was best for his life, he and I should be separated. That sentence scared me a lot since we had only been married for 6 months. And before we got married, we separated a few times because we couldn't understand each other at all, but soon after we came back because we still liked each other.

After I got married, I thought I would never go through a separation again, but what I didn't know was that the strength of my marriage was not in the fact that I got married, but in God as the Lord of our lives. We lived as Christians, but we had little to no concern or knowledge about the Kingdom of God, so like it says in Matthew 7:24-27, "Everyone who hears these words of mine and does them is like a wise man who built his house on the Rock. The rain fell, the flood came, and the winds beat against that house, but it did not collapse because it had been founded on the Rock. Everyone who hears these words of mine and does not do them is like a foolish man who built his house on sand. The rain fell, the flood came, and the winds beat against that house, and it collapsed; it was utterly destroyed!"

How did God change your situation, Nazik, as you sought Him wholeheartedly?

It was when I commented to a friend that I was going through some problems in my marriage that she encouraged me with the Word of God telling me that I had left the Lord. She said He was in second place in my life and for this reason God Himself was using a crisis in my marriage to call my attention to return to the arms of the Lord. She even gave me the following verse for me to meditate on: "May your happiness be in the Lord! He will give you what your heart desires." (Psalm 37:4)

That day was a watershed in my life, a turning point. I started SG (Seeking God) with all my heart in Christian books, the Bible, and with my prayers. Without realizing it, I put my work and my marriage above the Lord and it is logical that our Beloved is jealous of us and will never allow anything or anyone above Him. And we should be very happy that He uses our marriages to draw us closer to Him because it shows how much we are loved!

"Infidels, do you not understand that the friendship of the world is an enemy of God? Anyone who wants to be a friend of the world is an enemy of God, that he did dwell in us?" (James 4:2, 4-5)

A few days later our Beloved used a person who did not know anything about what I was going through, to tell me that I was to keep "fighting that He would be the center of my marriage." There my faith was established, and I decided to trust God. A big warning, beloved ones: I started my journey more than 2 years ago. And I fell and got up many times until I understood that the restoration of my life and my marriage was not a momentary issue but an eternal and constant journey. We have weaknesses in our flesh that can only be contained with a firm spiritual life in our relationship with Him, so don't be under the illusion that when the storm passes and your spouse returns home, you can relax, stop reading books, stop your courses, stop your daily devotionals, etc.

We all need to remain in continued spiritual growth so that our homes remain on the unshakable Rock that is our Beloved and HH (Heavenly Husband). "So whoever thinks he is standing is better to be careful not to fall." (1 Corinthians 10:12) "Therefore, whoever hears these words of mine and practices them is like a prudent man who built his house on the Rock. The rain fell, the rivers overflowed, the winds blew and hit that house, and it did not fall, because it had its foundations on the rock. But whoever hears these words of mine and does not practice them is like a fool who built his house on sand. The rain fell, the rivers overflowed, the winds blew and hit that house, and it fell. And her fall was great." (Matthew 7:24-27)

My EH (earthly husband) did not want our marriage anymore. He just didn't make the decision to leave the house because he didn't want to rush, but he treated me coldly, while I suffered and despaired. So I searched the internet for marriage restoration and that's when I found RMI. This ministry really taught me all the necessary truths that are in the Word of God regarding marriage.

I read Erin Thiele's book, How God Can and Will Restore Your Marriage. I read it many times and still read it today. Through this book that was written by someone who has been through what I went through and what you are going through, I learned to fight in the spirit and not in the flesh, although I still see that I need to be transformed every day.

After all, in fact, we don't have a crisis in marriage, we have a spiritual crisis just like Erin says. A crisis in our relationship with our Creator.

What principles, from God's Word (or through our resources), Nazik, did the Lord teach you during this trial?

In reading Erin's book I was able to be prepared to be a servant of the Lord, a pillar for my home. I learned that the world has its model of marriage, but this model does not sustain the relationship for long and always ends in pain. The world says that submission is a thing of the past, but beloved, nothing that is being taught in the Bible is passed, quite the contrary, the Word of God is renewed every day. Is it not true that the same verse cannot be interpreted in countless ways? "... each husband must love his wife as he loves himself, and each wife must respect her husband." (Ephesians 5:33) God made us in His image and likeness, so He knows us perfectly, and He already knew the possibility of our failures. In the above verse, God is not saying that only the man should love and only the woman must respect, He is only highlighting the areas in which both need more attention.

God has shown me that it is not by saying too much that I will be able to convince my EH to change anything that I know is wrong. I learned that I must listen to my husband when he asks me for something even though I don't see the need. Men and women were created differently and play different roles, but the husband supports the wife and the home and she assists her husband by giving that special touch that flourishes their lives. "So also you, wife, must obey your husband so that if he does not believe in the message of God, he will be led to believe by the way you act. honest and respectful." (1 Peter 3:1-2) "But I want you to understand that Christ has authority over every husband, that the husband has authority over his wife and that God has authority over Christ." (1 Corinthians 11:3) "For the husband has authority over the wife, just as Christ has authority over the Church. And Christ himself is the Savior of the Church, which is his body. Therefore, just as the Church is obedient to Christ, so the wife must obey her husband in everything." (Ephesians 5:23-24) "Then the Lord said: It is not good for man to live alone. I am going to make him someone to help him as if he were his other half." (Genesis 2:18)

In a nutshell, I learned the power of spiritual weapons such as faith, fasting, prayer, silence, and reading His Word. All these God-given weapons made it possible to cross the desert. There were many tears, but my HH kept me going when the struggles were too big and made me want to give up. It was very painful to go through the mill, but everything was the perfect plan from our Beloved to make me live in an abundance of happiness. I confess that at first I looked for and focused on my EH, but as time went on, I became much more concerned with pleasing my Lord, and that made all the difference. Our search must be only God who knows what we need, knows the right time for everything, knows what is good for us. We just need to trust.

What were the most difficult times that God helped you through, Nazik?

One of the lessons in the book How God Can and Will Restore Your Marriage talks about the reasons that lead our spouses to adultery. Reading about adultery in the book, I realized how long that chapter was, and then I asked myself, "Why am I reading so much about betrayal if it didn't happen?" Yes, beloved ones, it had happened! And God is so magnificent that He prepared me to know about this so I was able to be ready for the moment when my EH told me. My ground opened up when he told me of his adultery, but at the same time, I felt that I was being enveloped by a HUGE peace that alleviated my pain in a supernatural way. And I was able to immediately forgive him for that. In my normal state, I would never be able to forgive a betrayal right away, but this is how our Beloved does it. He does more than we can do. Beyond what we can even imagine. "Because if you forgive people who offend you, your Father in heaven will also forgive you." (Matthew 6:14) "Then Peter came close to Jesus and asked, 'Lord, how many times should I forgive my brother who sins against me? Seven times?' 'No!' He replied, 'You must not forgive seven times, but seventy-seven times.'" (Matthew 18:21-22)

Nazik, what was the "turning point" of your restoration?

One of the biggest reasons why God allows a marriage crisis is when we start to neglect His existence. When we allow work, conceited achievements, children, and husbands to come first in our lives God cares too much for us to not get our attention. Understand beloved ones: I am not saying that we should neglect our family and personal life. No, we must take care because all this is a blessing from the Lord, but none of this should be above God. The moment I understood this commandment, everything changed. I started to not care and not worry about my marriage restoration, the shame of separation, my college that was not finished, my debts, or anything else. I put EVERYTHING and everyone in the hands of the Master so that He could do EVERYTHING I could not do.

I began to seek God every day in His Word and in Love Songs fall in love with Him. I started to focus on making the Kingdom of God grow, giving love to others, helping anyone who needed help through the tools I had in my hands, and then I could be filled with peace. A peace that can only be divine, because for the reasons we are all living through it cannot be acquired, worked for, or earned.

After a while, I could understand that what motivated me to disobey the voice of God was my fear of losing my EH and for not recognizing that the God I had been looking for since I was 14 was the God who created heaven and the earth with the power of His voice! Nothing was impossible for Him. I realized how much this same God who created everything and even myself was everything I would need to live and have an abundant life with the love of His Son, my HH.

What we take into eternity is our relationship with the Lord. Our Beloved does not abandon us, does not sadden us, does not hurt us nor tell us lies. He is faithful, protects us, blesses us, and loves us. And loves a lot! "The Lord is a warrior; his name is Lord." (Exodus 15:3) "The Lord is my shepherd: I will lack nothing." (Psalm 23:1) "The Lord is good to all who trust in Him." (Lamentations 3:25) "The Lord is the only God; only God is our rock." (2 Samuel 22:32) "The Lord is kind and merciful, not easily angry, and very loving." (Psalm 103:8) "I know that the Lord is great; our God is above all gods." (Psalm 135:5) "The Lord is kind to all and cares for all his creatures with care." (Psalm 145:9) "But you, Lord, are God of compassion and love; you are always patient, kind and faithful." (Psalm 86:15) "But the Lord Jesus is faithful. He will give you strength and deliver you from the evil one." (Thessalonians 3:3)

Tell us HOW it happened, Nazik? Did your husband just walk in the front door? Nazik, did you suspect or could you tell you were close to being restored?

Within almost 5 years of our relationship, there were many comings and goings. And in one of those, I got involved with a random guy. Dear ones, it only feeds our flesh and needs for a short moment. We are left with so much pain from regret because we were with someone due to the pain we felt for the loss of those we really loved. So don't be pushed into something stupid. God has no one better than your EH for you, as well as no one better than you for Him. Rest in the Lord and do not act out of anger, disappointment, or hurt. We Christians must not follow our hearts. "Because we live by faith and not by what we see." (2 Corinthians 5:7) "Who can understand the human heart? There is nothing as deceiving as he is; he is too sick to be healed." (Jeremiah 17:9)

A year and a half after the beginning of my journey, a friend and I were visiting a church. I had let my church go at the beginning of my journey, and this commandment helped me focus on my personal restoration because I didn't have to worry about satisfying what the church or the fellow members thought was how I was supposed to follow the Lord for my life. Just asking for prayer makes people curious, and quick to give unwanted and most unbiblical advice and rumors are spread.

Well, while visiting this church, the Lord used a person to deliver a prophecy to me. This person said that I should trust in the restoration of my marriage because it was God who gave me my EH. A few weeks later my EH and I decided to meet to see each other and talk (we hadn't spoken for 2 months), so getting away from home and going out was a big thing.

When I decided to just trust the Lord and stop wanting things to be my way, everything was different. He became more calm and caring. I had asked God if it was His will, to restore our marriage before our wedding anniversary, and as I "delighted myself in Him" the Lord was very wonderful to hear my voice.

We spent our wedding anniversary like two lovebirds. When we returned, it was not an instant restoration and it has not been easy and it cost a lot until I understood that I should write my testimony because I, like many others, fantasized about a stereotype of restoration as in a fairytale, but we have seen that it is not so.

Today I see that we will be restored forever because every day we learn something new. My EH continued and continues to do things that sadden me. And because I am just as human, I am certainly doing things wrong. But I know that God is taking care of all things and the work that He started He will finish. "For I am sure that God, who began this good work in your life, will continue it until it is complete on the Day of Christ Jesus." (Philippians 1:6)

Would you recommend any of our resources in particular that helped you, Nazik?

Without a doubt! The emails that arrive every day with daily encouragement, the books A Wise Woman and How God Can and Will Restore Your Marriage are the foundation for every marriage. The courses, the ministry website, etc. All of this content has its foundation on His Word and everything most valuable that I started to do that started the process of restoring my marriage came from the Bible and this ministry through the materials mentioned above helped me to continue on my journey to this day.

Would you be interested in helping encourage other women, Nazik?

Yes of course! Just as I was helped, I wish to continue helping too. Only those who have passed through this valley or are still passing through will know how much we need someone who also trusts the Lord and put our Heavenly Husband first in our lives for our continued healing.

Either way, Nazik, what kind of encouragement would you like to leave women with, in conclusion?

Here at the RMI ministry, we each have received wonderful guidance on how to conduct our lives under God's obedience. I confess that I often heard the voice of God telling me to shut up and just pray and trust Him for everything, but I wanted to complain. And during each of the times when I did complain, it did absolutely nothing, quite the contrary, it only got worse.

Fights are not good for a marriage. How stupid the world is to say that? My EH and I never fight or disagree any more because being agreeable also means us remaining peaceful and trusting God to work it out.

So a piece of advice: don't complain about anything. Speak to your spouse in praise only, words that edify. We want that don't we? So give to others and He will make sure it's given to us! If there is something you would like to be different, ask God who can only change us. So treat him like a prince, just like you want to be treated like a princess.

Another very wonderful thing happened: in many prayers, I said that I loved God, but when I said that I had a lot of doubt. This was because I did not know our Beloved in my heart. I always had respect and prayed to Him from a young age as a God in heaven. But when I discovered that He is here, with me, closer than I could ever imagine, that's when I could say, "Darling, I love You! Thank You for Your infinite love. Thank You for giving me the chance to meet You."

Another very important fact too: FEAR NOTHING other than the Creator! There is nothing that escapes the control of His hands! The Bible says Do not fear 366 times. Isn't that amazing?! "So don't be afraid of anything. Everything that is covered will be discovered, and all that is hidden will be known." (Matthew 10:26) "Our help is in the name of the Lord, creator of heaven and earth." (Psalm 124:8) "Because your Creator is your Husband; the Lord of hosts is his name, and the Holy One of Israel is your Redeemer; He is called the God of all the earth." (Isaiah 54:5) "Isn't it true that two birds are sold for a few pennies? But none of them will fall to the ground if your Father doesn't let that happen." (Matthew 10:29)

Chapter 31

Alexis

"To sum up, all of you be harmonious, sympathetic, loving,
compassionate, and humble; not returning evil for evil
or insult for insult, but giving a blessing instead;
for you were called for the very purpose
that you would inherit a blessing."
—1 Peter 3:8-9

"Hypocritically I Accused My Husband When I was Involved with Someone"

Alexis, how did your Restoration Journey actually begin?

Before starting my journey, we had been married for 3 years and a half, and in that period we had already separated two times before—three separations in three years of marriage. Imagine everything you hear from relatives, friends, people who thought they had to give an opinion?

Since the beginning of our marriage, we have lived physically apart, because, due to his work, my EH (earthly husband) lived in another country. And I, because I was a public defender, I did not want to leave my job to follow him. Beloved, how it destroyed us! It was the stronghold for the enemy to take hold of my marriage and a lot of bad things happened.

When our daughter was born, I thought he would be more of a companion and be closer to me, to us. Another frustration that I blamed on my EH. I blamed everything on my EH, I became a bitter, contentious, doled-out tough love, and was a super jealous woman who did not know how to forgive. I was everything that the Word says about the foolish woman who tore her house down. Then, my EH left me, or rather, asked for a legal separation twice.

At first, he gave up right after a conversation we had about what was best for our daughter (emotional blackmail). In the second, he didn't want to know about me and it was right after his weight reduction surgery that he had. My EH said he wanted to enjoy life, and fighting with me was impossible, so he asked for the separation and went to live elsewhere rather than stay with us.

I still didn't know RMI, but I got very close to God. I prayed, fasted, did not look for my EH, although I followed his life on social networks. After two months, he looked for me and I had changed. Pure staging, nothing real. So, he returned home, but did not find a wise woman, on the contrary, she was the same foolish woman as before. It didn't take long for my EH to move out again, asking for a separation and this time contacting a lawyer. We fought a lot, we took offense at everything we said to one another, each contact was a hellish fight. I wanted another life, and in a way, I didn't want my marriage anymore. I called a cousin who is a lawyer to handle the divorce. As a result, I cultivated a lot more hatred and anger and told everyone who would listen. I was miserably unhappy.

I continued to follow his life on social media and it filled me with hatred for thinking that he was happy away from me and our daughter. This led to me having a relationship with someone else, but I was even more unhappy. Women are not meant to do this at all, it leaves a scar much more pronounced than it does for a man.

How did God change your situation, Alexis, as you sought Him wholeheartedly?

Even with a wall of hatred between us, one day, I searched the internet for testimonies of restored marriages, until I found RMI. At first, I didn't give much importance to what I'd found. I signed up to receive the devotionals and I barely read them. I purchased the book How God Can and Will Restore Your Marriage, but it took me weeks to start reading it. Until one day, I received an email from the ministry and scrolled the page until I found courses and read the first restored marriage in the course. So I decided to start reading the book. Beloved, each chapter was a beating in my heart. I was able to see myself in every word and identify my grave sins. I'm even ashamed to talk about the unbearable woman that I was and how hypocritical I was because I accused my husband of adultery, but I kept in touch with ex-boyfriends and I was still involved with one of them.

Oh my HH, how can you still love me? Then, after reading the book I started to apply the principles that Erin taught us, the first one being "letting go." I stopped following my EH on social networks. I also stopped repaying evil with evil but gave a blessing, "To sum up, all of you be harmonious, sympathetic, brotherly, kindhearted, and humble in spirit; not returning evil for evil or insult for insult, but giving a blessing instead; for you were called for the very purpose that you might inherit a blessing." 1 Peter 3:8-9 and I stopped all fighting with EH. During every contact we had, that he initiated, I treated him with respect and serenity. I did not show him "love" because the hate wall was up. I started to seek more and more to be the Bride that the Lord deserves, being in His presence and working on our intimacy because until then, the Lord for me was very distant. I didn't even see Him as a friend.

What principles, from God's Word (or through our resources), Alexis, did the Lord teach you during this trial?

Mainly "letting go"; and also to give EVERYTHING to the Lord and rest in His love, trusting God to restore my marriage.

What were the most difficult times that God helped you through, Alexis?

It was very difficult when my EH sought me out for intimate matters through the internet, since he was in another state, and then he disappeared and I wouldn't talk to me for days and it would kill me inside making me feel used. But once I did it as "unto the Lord" and later remembered that He was my Lover, the shame disappeared and surprisingly, my EH stopped humiliating me this way!

Alexis, what was the "turning point" of your restoration?

Over time, my EH started talking to me more and talking about work, his routine. I realized that he was very tired because his work was consuming him beyond normal. He also confided in me that he was using medicines that stimulate concentration and kept him awake for days. I started to pray more for my EH, begging our HH (Heavenly Husband) to take care of him, not to allow the use of drugs, and to keep people who did him harm from His son's life. I was no longer wondering if there was OW (other woman), I started to be very concerned about his health and wellbeing, but I didn't say anything. I just took my concerns to the Lord. One day, he was very ill and was rushed to the hospital. Beloved, my husband took a lot of the medicine and stayed awake for 3 days working beyond what his body can handle that led to his breakdown.

Tell us HOW it happened, Alexis? Did your husband just walk in the front door? Alexis, did you suspect or could you tell you were close to being restored?

In short, after being discharged, my EH took the first plane he could and returned home for good. We had not discussed what he will do for work, but when he arrived in our city he came straight to our home. I didn't ask anything, we were intimate and he continued to stay, staying longer and longer content with the peacefulness of our home and the new me.

As Erin says, after the husband's return home, our situation often gets even worse than we had on our journey. I had to control myself a lot to obey my EH, not to argue, not to feel needy, because he did not return loving and full of love. Just broken.

Often, I still feel distant emotionally so I am even more grateful to have a Lover who gives me everything I need. Nothing is perfect, except our HH. Sometimes I fail to follow the principles, but the Lord uses these to draw my attention back to doing my lessons and He leads me back to His path.

Beloved, the Lord took my EH to begin working with people who have families, men who respect their homes and have positively influenced my EH. I am so thankful to the Lord so much for this grace, because before my husband was working with young people, who were uncommitted, with risky, nasty habits. Anyway, that was another wonderful blessing that our Beloved gave me after restoration. It still amazes me that I was once so hypocritical that I accused my husband when I was involved with someone!

Would you recommend any of our resources in particular that helped you, Alexis?

Not just some, but EVERY ONE of your resources!! The book How God can and will restore your marriage was the key that made me want to go find and meet our Lord. In addition to the books, the courses have also been instrumental in my restoration as a person.

Would you be interested in helping encourage other women, Alexis?

Really interested!

Either way, Alexis, what kind of encouragement would you like to leave women with, in conclusion?

Trust in the Lord and only Him, for as the Holy Scriptures say: "What no one has ever seen or heard, and what no one ever thought could happen, this is what God has prepared for those who love Him" (1 Corinthians 2:9) This was the verse that accompanied me through one the most difficult moments during my journey and that I still meditate today. Even in the worst of situations, dear friends, the Lord does not leave us and He wants to help you, not only by restoring marriages but also by restoring families, you as a person, and help you find your personal relationship with Him. I love You, my Beloved.

Chapter 32

Elke

"Wait for the Lord and keep His way,
And He will exalt you to inherit the land;
When the wicked are eliminated, you will see it."
—Psalms 37:34

"I Had an Online Affair"

Elke, how did your Restoration Journey actually begin?

I had an online affair with an old friend 20 yrs. into my 2nd marriage. For over two years my tormented husband tried all he could to change things and fix the things that had hurt me over the years, but the devil was happily in control to the point I believed I could have a double life. What I didn't know was, my husband had prayed the hedge of thorns around me and sure enough over time, my "lover fled" but it was not soon enough for my husband. He gave up his fight as the other man fled and began to stay gone on weekends. I went to marriage counseling and was told it can't be done alone. So I searched online to know "how one person could save a marriage" as I returned to God with a broken & contrite heart. Somehow I found Erin in one of those searches over 12 years ago.

How did God change your situation, Elke, as you sought Him wholeheartedly?

He showed me all the bitterness I had. He broke my heart more in regards to divorcing my first husband. I was brought to total repentance. I went to my first child and asked for forgiveness. I asked if she felt I should return to her father but she asked me not to as she didn't want her step brother and sister to have them in the same situation and her children knew only my current husband as Papaw and she didn't want to confuse them. So I called and asked my first husband for forgiveness instead. God sent me angels to my work place. Women who knew His power and had encouragement. I began to see I could go on alone if that was His plan.

What principles, from God's Word (or through our resources), Elke, did the Lord teach you during this trial?

How to wait on Him. Seeing my wrongs (so many of them!). To REPENT, wait...wait some more. Praise God for every circumstance. Give Him my tears. Not to speak of our situation to others, only to God.

What were the most difficult times that God helped you through, Elke?

The fear of failing, the heartbreak of knowing I had no good witness for my husband to trust. Being without human companionship at night or during a blizzard (our children were grown)! Trying to cover for Papaw's absence when he was gone (without bitterness since I was the one to blame).

Elke, what was the "turning point" of your restoration?

My husband wanted to leave but he was out of work for winter. And because we lived in my parent's apartment building, he couldn't tell me to leave. His plan was to go as soon as he had work. He began to separate our finances...different banks for his unemployment and another for my pay. As I prayed God brought RAIN...lots of it! Day after day it didn't stop! Mind you, I was not asking for rain to start...but as I saw what it was allowing to happen, I began to pray for God to use it to give us more time to heal! Depression set in for my earthly husband and God gave me the opportunity to minister to his needs while making it clear I was repentant.

Tell us HOW it happened, Elke? Did your husband just walk in the front door?

The weather finally broke and he was getting called back to work. In passing I asked if he would consider staying. He said he would think about it. It was 5 months before our 24th wedding anniversary. I took on a second job and offered to help pay any bills to make it easier for him. I stuck to the payments he gave to me and showed I could be trusted (I had ruined our finances in the years of the affair). Our healing was a matter of him trusting me slowly. And I knew this would be the way of it because of my unfaithfulness.

Elke, did you suspect or could you tell you were close to being restored?

During this time, I viewed any indication of positivity coming from my husband "a God stop." They increased more and more. I praised God constantly. There began to be peace in the days and he just stayed. I refused to let fear of failure haunt me since I knew God's promises and the forgiveness I had learned to walk in. I rebuked the evil one as he tried to bring up my failures.

Would you recommend any of our resources in particular that helped you, Elke?

How God can and will restore your marriage, Wise Woman, By the Word of Their Testimony.

Elke do you have favorite Bible verses that you would like to pass on to women reading your Testimonies? Promises that He gave you, Elke?

"Wait on the Lord, and keep His way, and He shall exalt you to inherit the land; when the wicked are cut off, you shall see it." Psalms 37:34 NKJV

This verse was very important to me as we had never had our own home—after we were restored, my husband began looking for the home we live in now!

Would you be interested in helping encourage other women, Elke?

Yes, by my giving.

Either way, Elke, what kind of encouragement would you like to leave women with, in conclusion?

God forgives and heals those who fall before Him and surrender all. If your husband is not a believer, give him completely to God and be willing to wait. Don't quit seeking God and trusting Him.

Chapter 33

Varvara

"He will not fear bad news;
His heart is steadfast, trusting in the Lord."
—Psalm 112:7

"My Husband is Involved with Another Woman and She's Pregnant"

Varvara, how did your Restoration Journey actually begin?

It all started in December when my husband told me that he wanted a separation because he couldn't live with me anymore. When he said that, I already imagined that he was with an OW (other woman) because for some months he was distant. At the time our daughter was just a year old and he was always in love with the baby and such an excellent father. That's when I realized that about 3 mouths prior to him asking for the separation, he was emotionally distant from us, played very little with our daughter, arrived home late, found reasons to argue every day, and compulsively gambled on the internet.

I spent the rest of December and the first half of January very distressed. At that time he traveled a lot, saying it was for work, and every Saturday when he got back home, all he wanted to talk about was the end of our marriage. His heart was already very, very far from me; until one Saturday in late January, I was shocked when he said he wanted to continue with our marriage.

Another week passed and when he returned from a trip he called me at his parents' house to confess that he had become involved with a woman and she was pregnant. I was devastated. I thought I had entered a parallel world he ended the conversation by saying he would only come home to get his things. When he came he tried to talk about coming home but I was adamant, in my self-righteousness, I was sure I couldn't be with a man who did this to me.

Two weeks after the separation I already had a good lawyer and the divorce papers were being prepared. The following week while the divorce papers were being prepared, I went to visit my old church, and there I met an old friend. I told her what had happened. She told me she did not believe in divorce and said she would ask for a friend of hers, who was participating in a marriage restoration ministry (RMI) to contact me. That same night, the girl (who today is my dear friend and ePartner) sent me the link to the ministry and gave me some information.

I really wanted a divorce but my Beloved spoke to my heart (Glory to His Infinite Love) or "Glory to His Infinite Love" and told me I was not to give up. As I read about the ministry and actually spent the entire night reading, without understanding much, I went ahead and filled out the marriage questionnaire and started taking course 1 that night.

How did God change your situation, Varvara, as you sought Him wholeheartedly?

My Beloved, Prince of my life, was very kind and generous and loving to me. He was always so patient with me. I was very hard at heart, based every decision on my self-righteousness, belief in feminism, but with each lesson, I came into conflict with myself. I thought about giving up thousands of times, but He was patient and was shaping my heart day after day.

After the first month and a half of separation, in the midst of many tears, I saw how contentious I was and I surrendered fully at His feet. My attitude instantly changed! I became less harsh and more grateful to the Lord and my faith in His purpose became visible. People I knew started to comment on how I was so at peace, how I was happier. And little by little I was being introduced to my closest friend my true Love who gave me so much peace in the midst of so many adversities that happened.

What principles, from God's Word (or through our resources), Varvara, did the Lord teach you during this trial?

Just like every restored marriage testimony I've read, "letting go" and "God is in control" and "submission to the husband" were certainly the principles that the Lord taught me the most and were the most difficult—needing much more of Him than I had. These verses were the ones that guided me all the time. "But seek first the kingdom of

God, and his righteousness, and all these things will be added to you."
Matthew 6:33 "Like streams of water so is the king's heart in the hand
of the LORD, who inclines to all your will." Proverbs 21:1

**What were the most difficult times that God helped you through,
Varvara?**

The most difficult moment was when the Lord told me that I should
stop the divorce. I suffered a lot, very much, and after a week of
wrestling with Him, I dismissed the lawyer and asked the Lord that if
He really wanted my husband to contact me, then He would need to do
it.

Two days after this prayer, my husband called me and I told him that I
could not continue the divorce. That's when I said I had already
dismissed her. He was amazed and shocked and then asked why. I was
prepared with a response after meditating on "But sanctify Christ as
Lord in your hearts, always being ready to make a defense to everyone
who asks you to give an account of the hope that is in you, yet with
gentleness and reverence." 1 Peter 3:15

I replied gently saying that my God did not want me to continue with
the divorce but if he wanted to continue I would agree with him. He
hung up and minutes later he called me and said he would continue to
pursue divorce because as soon as he had financial means, he would be
living with the OW (other woman).

This was yet another very painful moment that happened, which
continued after our restoration when he checked the child's DNA and
found that it was his son. I suffered a lot, and in the following months,
it took a lot out of me. But God in His mercy again calmed my heart
and has been working on this situation for good. I will share more in
future praise reports.

Varvara, what was the "turning point" of your restoration?

The turning point was when I really poured myself out to the Lord when
He became my true Husband after reading the first two Abundant Life
books. I understood that if I were in the center of His will, and my heart
was for only Him, then the best would happen, everything for my good.

"And we know that God causes all things to work together for good to those who love God, to those who are called according to His purpose." Romans 8:28

I suppose it was when I let it go completely. When I didn't even think about the restoration. At this stage, I just wanted the restoration because I understood that He has a purpose because I didn't even want to be restored anymore. My husband told me that when I told him that I could not continue the divorce, it was when God began to deal with him, in his deception and he started to have days filled with conflict and to see that he was in sin.

Tell us HOW it happened, Varvara? Did your husband just walk in the front door? Varvara, did you suspect or could you tell you were close to being restored?

We were separated for 6 months when my husband and I got back together. During this time, I had no contact with him, I neither wanted nor allowed him to contact me in the beginning. At the end of July, my daughter turned 2 and my parents and I decided to have a party for her but I didn't want to invite him. At the insistence of my father, and finally after understanding about respect for authority, I obeyed my father and in June I had my first conversation with my husband, saying that he was welcome to come to the party.

This, I later found out, is when the horrific fights with OW started. When he decided to come and told her she could not come along. On the first weekend of July, my husband was sitting on the sofa in our living room saying that he wanted to come home but he needed to resolve the situation with the OW. It was at that point he started coming home every weekend, and it was very pleasant because God had already shaped me a lot and I was no longer contentious. When he left, I was delighted (not focusing on who he was returning to) because I needed my time with my own Lover!

Would you recommend any of our resources in particular that helped you, Varvara?

Each of the RMI courses and videos are channels of the Lord to minister in our lives. The books RYM and both Abundant Life books were instruments in healing my brokenness.

Would you be interested in helping encourage other women, Varvara?

Yes

Either way, Varvara, what kind of encouragement would you like to leave women with, in conclusion?

There is no better place to be than in the arms of our Beloved Heavenly Husband. Everything has a purpose and He has everything in His control no matter how you feel. Keep going, even when storms arise and rock you to the core. It happens to all of us but there is no safer place than to remain near it. "You will not fear bad news; your heart is steadfast, trusting in the Lord." Psalm 112:7

Dear Lord, as I write the end of my testimony, it seems that I smell Your hair, I feel myself leaning against Your chest, my Love. Thank You my Beloved for being beautiful and loving us all as unique and special.

Chapter 34

Mandy

"Now faith is the certainty of things
hoped for, a proof of things not seen."
—Hebrews 11:1

"Giving My God-Given Advantage
Over to the OW"

Mandy, how did your Restoration Journey actually begin?

In October, after only 3 years of marriage and having a 4-year-old daughter, I realized that my husband no longer prioritized his family. It was during this month that he spent the first night away from home. Three months later we separated and that's when I discovered the existence of another woman. Then after confronting him (that I know is a huge mistake and gives our God-given advantage over to the Other Woman), is when I heard words my Heavenly Husband never designed anyone to hear! He said he was in love with her (and I made my next mistake) when I said I refused to let him go to be with any woman!

How did God change your situation, Mandy, as you sought Him wholeheartedly?

In the beginning, I was sure that my marriage was no longer possible, it was best to separate. But the real suffering started in my life because I found myself alone. My daughter cried a lot for her father's absence and I had no one who could help me. No one tells you this when they're all telling you to separate.

It was then that I started to seek God, I asked for strength to survive so much pain. However, while searching for God, all my mistakes and sins in relation to my marriage came to me. So I suffered, even more, when God revealed to me that I was just as guilty of the failure of our marriage as my husband. At this stage, my husband was already very involved with the Other Woman. In my desperation, I went on the internet in search of something that would guide me and help me survive. It was then that God showed me the RMI site and I read the book How God can and will restore your marriage practically all the way through on the same day.

What principles, from God's Word (or through our resources), Mandy, did the Lord teach you during this trial?

Through the books and each of the courses, I learned that there is God's perfect time for everything in our lives. So I started to pray to ask God to be able to have the patience to wait for God to take action. There was one certainty in my heart: God did not want my marriage to end. So I trusted in God's promises and especially in the "win without a word" that told my heart that I could see my husband back without having to say anything to him and instead speak to God only about everything.

What were the most difficult times that God helped you through, Mandy?

In the midst of all this, a lot of sad things happened. First, my husband started to travel with Other Woman and to go along with this, since he was always gone, he did not give the necessary assurance to our daughter who was devastated that her daddy was gone and had no time to spend with her.

The other shock was when the Other Woman called me to ask for a divorce so she could marry him. My Earthly Husband even came to my house to scold me, calling me vile names while the Other Woman was there grinning.

Each time, the Lord spoke to me to trust Him more and make sure that every day, to give myself ample time to have my moment of intimacy with Him. He helped me every time and always drew me closer to Him. I always cried alone with my Heavenly Husband and felt His arms comforting me.

Mandy, what was the "turning point" of your restoration?

After three years in this situation with nothing happening, always seeking peace with my husband by winning without a word, things started to change. The Other Woman was becoming uncontrollable. She was jealous to the point of breaking everything at my mother-in-law's house where my husband lived. My mother-in-law witnessed everything and told her son, my Earthly Husband, she would not accept the situation anymore and he would have to move out. At this point, my husband decided that he did not want to live in that relationship anymore so he just told her to get out.

Tell us HOW it happened, Mandy? Did your husband just walk in the front door? Mandy, did you suspect or could you tell you were close to being restored?

My husband was gradually approaching me to begin a friendship, inviting us to go on a vacation, a trip we had talked about taking for years. And after that, we began getting closer every day. Soon after he broached the conversation about us moving back in together. Then he decided we needed a fresh start, so he began renovating a new house we should be moving into soon.

Would you recommend any of our resources in particular that helped you, Mandy?

The books: How God can and will restore your marriage and A wise woman, the online courses are wonderful and Erin's videos have been a huge part in my journey to trust Him.

Would you be interested in helping encourage other women, Mandy?

Yes

Either way, Mandy, what kind of encouragement would you like to leave women with, in conclusion?

Trust in the Lord, ask for His advice, and seek Him with an open heart. No matter what you are SEEING or experiencing TRUST GOD BECAUSE HE IS ACTING on your behalf EVEN WITHOUT YOU SEEING that anything is happening.

Chapter 35

Amber

"Love the Lord your God with all your heart
and with all your soul and with all your
mind and with all your strength."
—Mark 12:30

"I Demanded Sex"

Amber, how did your Restoration Journey actually begin?

Almost 4 years ago, I met the man who is now my EH (earthly husband) through a friend from work. When I saw him I was not attracted to him, but something caught my attention in him, a light shone on him. I did not recognize that he was the light of the Lord, for he was already an evangelical and a man fearing God. Over the months we got closer we started dating and fell in love. He invited me to attend services and I went with him. At the time I considered myself a non-practicing Catholic. After 4 months of dating, we fell into sin, started to become intimate, on his initiative, and continued our relationship in fornication. Months before we were married, I decided to be baptized in an evangelical church, but not out of faith in the Lord but to please my future husband. He promised me a wonderful life, loyalty, financial support, he was loving and making plans to live with me the way I dreamed. I started to love him more than anything and everyone. We were married 7 months after my baptism.

I thought that my happiness depended on my EH (and I yearned to live everything he promised me. After 1 month of marriage, my EH changed his behavior towards me. He didn't pay attention to me and marriage was not his priority, he no longer followed the biblical teachings. I started to pressure him because I no longer felt loved by him and confronted him. I became contentious, quarrelsome, eavesdropping, cynical, arrogant, jealous, controlling, accused him of his sins, judged him. I covered everything he promised me before we got married, including I demanded sex because I wanted to have children and our situation got worse every day. I talked about divorce at every fight, he always remained calm, but cold. I even drafted a consensual divorce petition for him to sign, with some legal conditions, for a consensual divorce directly at the civil registry office, but the Lord prevented him from signing, glory to God, and my EH (earthly husband) started paying attention to me.

After a few days he started to offend and humiliate me because I was unemployed, and soon he stopped providing me financially. By forcing him, he literally despised me, he didn't speak to me for days, he kicked me out of the apartment several times and I got more and more contentious. I tried the silent treatment, played the game of "tough love", so much that it reflected in my relationships with other people. I treated them badly! And that's when I realized that I had no relationship with God. I went to the services troubled, murmuring, blaming my earthly husband and God for my unhappiness. I mistakenly decided to seek the help of a couple of pastors from the church we attended, and ultimately exposed my marriage and my husband, talked about his sins, and acted as if I were a victim.

When my husband agreed to do "Christian therapy" I was so hopeful that I was thrilled to think he was going to change. But after therapy I started to rebel against my husband again because I didn't see any changes in him, he was worse for me. In a moment I lost patience with him and physically attacked him, I took all my anger out on him. As he didn't react to my physical aggressions that day, I realized that I was the wrong one, I felt terrible. My situation was serious and impossible to resolve.

How did God change your situation, Amber, as you sought Him wholeheartedly?

I decided not to tell anyone else about my situation after that huge mistake and one day I went online to look for marriage testimonies and God guided me right to the RMI website. Reading everything on the site and then finding the book How God Can and Will Restore Your Marriage I discovered that it was I who was a Pharisee, that I only saw the sins of others, was not respectful and not submissive to my EH, I saw a fool who destroyed her home. I was scared and disgusted with myself, I didn't want to be like that. For 3 months I started the online course and read the book because the enemy made me believe that the RMI was a fairytale. But the Lord reminded me of this ministry every day but I resisted. Until one day I was alone at home and it made me want to read the book, when I started I couldn't stop reading!

I would panic because the principles confronted me, and at the same time, I was in tears crying out to the Lord for His forgiveness, mainly for having baptized me without loving Him. Then I realized that everything I was going through had the Lord's permission in order for me to see and desire Him, "But I have it against you that you left your first love" (Rev. 2:4). After the biblical principles taught by RMI, I repented and asked the Lord for forgiveness and reconciled with Him, I came to know my Heavenly Husband, His Grace, to love and adore Him.

What principles, from God's Word (or through our resources), Amber, did the Lord teach you during this trial?

I started meditating on His Word and praying daily, I started to have a true relationship with My Beloved, a relationship that I didn't know existed. Not once at church did I ever hear this was possible. When I met my HH (Heavenly Husband), the scales fell from my eyes, I saw the truth, "And you will know the truth, and the truth will set you free." (John 8:32). I also talked with my earthly husband and asked for forgiveness for being so unfair to him, so contentious, and he forgave me. My relationship with my earthly husband improved immediately, it matured. But even so, I fell into temptation and rebelled against him again because He tested and hardened my EH heart for me. God knew I was just focusing on winning him back and I stopped focusing on my HH. I was struggling in my own strength and I forgot that the Lord is fighting for me, as He guarantees in His Word that "The king's heart is like channels of water in the hand of the Lord; He turns it wherever He pleases." (Prov. 21:1).

Well, would you believe once again, as I "let go" of my Heavenly Husband and did not "let go" of my earthly husband, I again disagreed with everything my EH (earthly husband) said and did?! I went back to being contentious. And yet the Lord continued to be merciful to me, glory to the name of the Lord, because I had difficulties in applying biblical principles, all of them, mainly "letting go" and "winning without words". If I should say, "My foot has slipped," Your faithfulness, Lord, will support me. When my anxious thoughts multiply within me, Your comfort delights my soul." (Ps 94:18-19), the Lord was faithful, just and supported me, gave me comfort and taught me each principle as I continued praying, confessing my sins and waiting on Him. I learned to accept that the Lord's will is sovereign and "died" to myself, that was the key to my recovery.

What were the most difficult times that God helped you through, Amber?

First, I had to learn to live the first commandment of the Lord: "You will therefore love the Lord your God with all your heart and with all your soul and with all your understanding and with all your strength; it is the first commandment" (Mark 12:30). Then, "And the second, similar to this, is: You shall love your neighbor as yourself. There is no other commandment greater than these" (Mark 12:31).

When I couldn't really repent, because repentance, which is essential to true conversion, involves dying to sin. The Bible compares repentance to the Lord's death and resurrection. There has to be a radical lifestyle change. The Bible uses terms such as "killing the old man" and putting on the new. It describes in detail the exact changes that need to be made (Eph 4: 17-32; Col. 3). Bad habits - strife, sexual immorality, lying, greed, anger, pride, etc. - need to be eliminated from life itself, while the fruits of the Holy Spirit, which is "love, joy, peace, longsuffering, kindness, goodness, faith, meekness, temperance", must be added (Gal. 5:22).

This is the result of regret that I was unable to have, so it was very difficult, but the Lord was merciful to me and taught me that my relationship with Him is eternal, permanent, and perfect. He could transform me if I really wanted to walk in His ways. I learned to love Him and I am working to always preserve our relationship to be the best of my life. All the trials, tribulations, struggles that I went through and passed are blessings for me, because I found the true meaning of my life, loving the Lord. Faith worked on me, took away my anxiety, glory to God! The Lord has transformed me so much that people notice. I am happy, even though my earthly marriage is still not as I wished it was, but God knows I still have many more wonderful changes to make in me and my earthly husband too! Blessed is the Lord.

Amber, what was the "turning point" of your restoration?

When I gave my life to my HH (Heavenly Husband), as My Lord and Savior, and Lover. Today I understand that we are all experiencing a spiritual war, I know that our struggle is not against our husbands or anyone else. That to be happy we depend exclusively on God to do it. For us to have good health, children, employment, goods, for everything we depend on the sovereign will of God. And I understand that without the Lord, as our Heavenly Husband, Savior of our lives, it is impossible for an earthly husband and an earthly wife to gather sufficient strength, having feelings of love, or good intentions to fulfill biblical principles and enter into marriage. But because of the Lord, two sinners, a man, and a woman, completely different individuals, can be miraculously transformed into one. Earthly marriage is a piece of heaven on Earth!

Tell us HOW it happened, Amber? Did your husband just walk in the front door? Amber, did you suspect or could you tell you were close to being restored?

My EH (earthly husband) never left our home, despite the fact that he had every reason to leave, but I confess that it made my restoration difficult, as we spent days without speaking and it was an embarrassing situation. I suspected that God was restoring our marriage when I started being obedient and submissive to Him and my EH being loving and kind to me. My EH also began to seek the face of the Lord and to want to be intimate with me. He talked to me about my changes and asked me how I managed to change, what was the reason for my change and I was able to tell him there were the same materials for the men.

Would you recommend any of our resources in particular that helped you, Amber?

I recommend all the materials available. In particular, I took the online courses (1, 2 and 3), ordered and read the paperback book How God Can and Will Restore Your Marriage that I found helpful. I read the daily encouragements every day, watched the Be E videos many times, read all the testimonies (ordering the eBook packet), and keep up daily readings of Psalms and Proverbs. Thanks to Erin and all the RMI partners who provide us with these precious materials, may God continue to bless them!

Would you be interested in helping encourage other women, Amber?

Yes

Either way, Amber, what kind of encouragement would you like to leave women with, in conclusion?

"But seek first the kingdom of God and his righteousness, and all these things will be added to you" (Matt. 6:33). Please do not exchange peace, salvation, eternal life, love, happiness, deliverance from the world of sins, which only the Lord can offer you, for the pleasures that the world provides us are empty and fleeting. The Lord knows our needs, He knows everything we need to live in this world, so "This is what the Lord says: "Cursed is the man who trusts in mankind And makes flesh his strength, And whose heart turns away from the Lord. For he will be like a bush in the desert, And will not see when prosperity comes, But will live in stony wastes in the wilderness, A land of salt that is not inhabited. Blessed is the man who trusts in the Lord, And whose trust is the Lord. For he will be like a tree planted by the water That extends its roots by a stream, And does not fear when the heat comes; But its leaves will be green, And it will not be anxious in a year of drought, Nor cease to yield fruit." (Jer 17:5-8) With this testimony, I thank God and this Ministry! May only the name of the Lord be praised, amen

What you have read is just a *small sample* of the POWER and FAITHFULNESS of God that are told through countless restored marriages! We continue to post new restored marriage, and restored relationship testimonies (children, siblings, parents, etc.) on our site each week.

Don't let ANYONE try to convince you that God cannot restore YOUR marriage! It is a lie. The TRUTH is that He is MORE THAN ABLE!!

Is Your Marriage... Crumbling? Hopeless? Or Ended in Divorce?

At Last There's Hope!

Have you been searching for marriage help online? It's not by chance, nor is it by coincidence, that you have this book in your hands. God is leading you to Restore Ministries that began by helping marriages that *appear* hopeless—like yours!

God has heard your cry for help in your marriage struggles and defeats. He predestined this **Divine Appointment** to give you the hope that you so desperately need right now!

We know and understand what you are going through since many of us in our restoration fellowship have a restored marriage and family! No matter what others have told you, your marriage is not hopeless! We know, after filling almost two books of restored marriage testimonies, that God is able to restore any marriage—especially yours!

"Behold, I am the LORD, the God of all flesh; is anything too difficult for Me?" (Jeremiah 32:27).

If you have been told that your marriage is hopeless or that without your husband's help your marriage cannot be restored! Each week we post a new Restored Relationship from one of our Restoration Fellowship Members that we post on our site.

"Ah Lord GOD! Behold, You have made the heavens and the earth by Your great power and by Your outstretched arm! Nothing is too difficult for You"! (Jeremiah 32:17).

If you have been crying out to God for more help, someone who understands, someone you can talk to, then we invite you to join our

RMI Restoration Fellowship. Since beginning this fellowship, we have seen more marriages restored on a regular basis than we ever thought possible!

Restoration Fellowship

Restoration is a "narrow road"—look around, most marriages end in divorce! But if your desire is for a restored marriage, then our Restoration Fellowship is designed especially for you!

Since beginning this fellowship, we have seen marriages restored more consistently than we ever thought possible.

Let us help you stay committed to "working with God" to restore your marriages. Restoration Fellowship can offer you the help, guidance, and support you will need to stay on the path that leads to victory—*your* marriage restored!

Let us assure you that all of our marriages were restored by GOD (through His Word) as we sought Him to lead us, teach us, guide us and transform us through His Holy Spirit. This, too, is all you need for *your* marriage to be restored.

However, God continues to lead people to our ministry and fellowship to gain the faith, support and help that so many say that they needed in their time of crisis.

"Being introduced to this ministry, I know it was through God and His divine appointment. I say this because even though I have been a Christian since I was 5 years old, I was about to give up on my marriage, because in the churches apparently they do not give so much importance to this subject and for this reason we see more and more the enemy destroying homes and ministries even the marriages of pastors.

It is true!! God can and will restore your marriage, everyone must read the book, take the courses, see the truths contained entirely in the Word and compare it to what people in the church say. You will often find that what you believed and what the church says does not match what God has for our lives and that following these commandments will cause you to be seen as crazy. But one thing is certain, what God has promised us, He will fulfill, as long as we follow HIS ways.

As I said, I have been a Christian since I was 5 years old. I had seen several family seminars even before I got married. So I was always at the church, but some subjects always seemed strange to me, especially this one about marriage. I always saw couples who broke up and it seemed that the church did not give any importance to that or it was just judgments for both involved. It was through these courses / books that I came to understand more about God's will for our lives and I am willing to spread this truth starting from the community where I live.

I thank God for having sent my wife's friend to present the RYM book to me at a time when I was about to give up and with that I was able to clearly see God's care in my life and HIS restoration process." Rubens in Brazil

"When I found RMI, I was on month 3 of my husband out of the house. I felt like I had tried everything to win him back. Let him be, be nice, try to convince him to come back, all of the things that I learned that you shouldn't do. I thought I controlled the situation. And none of it was helping. He was bringing up divorce and filing papers, selling our house, etc. Granted those things are still being brought up. I have learned so much in the last 30 days and have more hope than I have had in a while." Tammy in Texas

"I was suicidal and in deep pain. I felt so alone and hopeless. I decided to fast and during that time I changed and things were looking up and that's when I saw your link on a standers FB Comments thread. (How ironic) And that's when my life changed and I saw how wrong I was how contentious and revolting. And I am doing everything I can to change me and AIA have asked God to not leave any of the old me. That I want to be completely transformed in His image. My relationship with my husband is peaceful now. We are no longer attacking each other. There is mutual respect and consideration which is so far off, from where we were a few months ago." Valerie in Sri Lanka

Join our Restoration Fellowship TODAY and allow us to help YOU **restore** YOUR marriage.

HopeAtLast.com

Like What You've Read?

By the Word of Their Testimony Series
on EncouragingBookstore.com & Amazon.com

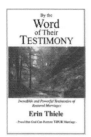

Word of Their Testimony (Book 1): Incredible and Powerful Testimonies of Restored Marriages

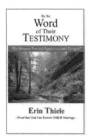

Word of Their Testimony (Book 2): No Weapon Formed Against you will Prosper

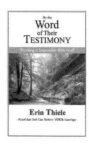

By the Word of Their Testimony (Book 3): Nothing is Impossible With God

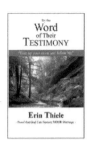 Word of Their Testimony (Book 4): Take up your cross and follow Me

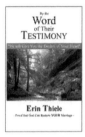 Word of Their Testimony (Book 5): He will Give You the Desires of Your Heart

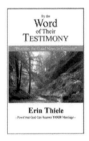 Word of Their Testimony (Book 6): Proclaim the Good News to Everyone

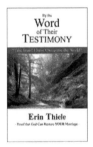 Word of Their Testimony (Book 7): Take Heart! I have Overcome the World

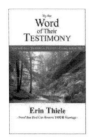

Word of Their Testimony (Book 8): You will have Treasure in Heaven—Come, follow Me

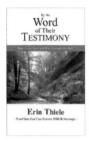

Word of Their Testimony (Book 9): Rest in the Lord and Wait Patiently for Him: eBook

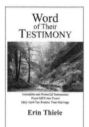

Word of Their Testimony: Incredible and Powerful Testimonies of Restored Marriages From Men

Also Available

Our Abundant Life Series
on EncouragingBookstore.com & Amazon.com

 Finding the Abundant Life

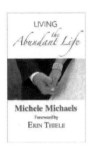 Living the Abundant Life

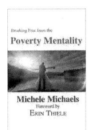 Breaking Free from the Poverty Mentality

 Moving Mountains by Michele Michaels

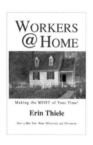 Workers @ Home: Making the MOST of Your Time!

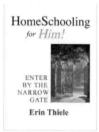 Home Schooling for Him: Enter by the Narrow Gate

Please visit our Websites where you'll also find these books as FREE Courses for women

Our Restore Series
on EncouragingBookstore.com & Amazon.com

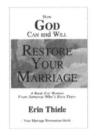

How God Can and Will Restore Your
Marriage: From Someone Who's Been There

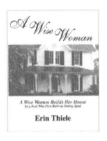

A Wise Woman: A Wise Woman Builds Her
House By a FOOL Who First Built on Sinking
Sand

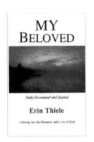

My Beloved: Daily Devotional and Journal
Coming into the Presence and Love of God

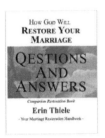

How God Will Restore Your Marriage:
Questions and Answers

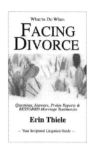

What to Do When Facing Divorce

Facing Divorce, Again: Enthusiastically and without Fear

Please visit our Websites where you'll also find these books as FREE Courses for women.

For our Men

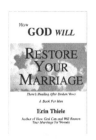

How God Will Restore Your Marriage:
There's Healing After Broken Vows — A
Book for Men

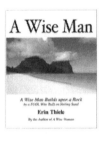

A Wise Man: A Wise Man Builds Upon a
Rock by a FOOL Who Built on Sinking Sand

Each of our books is available on one of our websites as
FREE Courses!

Restore Ministries International

POB 830 Ozark, MO 65721 USA
For more help
Please visit one of our Websites:

EncouragingWomen.org

HopeAtLast.com

LoveAtLast.org

RestoreMinistries.net

Aidemaritale.com (French)

AjudaMatrimonial.com (Portuguese)

AmoreSenzaFine.com (Italian)

AyudaMatrimonial.com (Spanish)

Eeuwigdurendeliefde-nl.com (Dutch)

EvliliginiKurtar.com (Turkish)

EternalLove-jp.com (Japanese)

Pag-asa.org (Tagalog)

Uiteindelikhoop.com (Afrikaans)

Zachranamanzelstva.com (Slovak)

Wiecznamilosc.com (Polish)

EncouragingMen.org